The Broken Sixpence

The Broken Sixpence

Maggie Turrell

Copyright © 2013 by Neville Hodgson.

ISBN: Softcover   978-1-4836-8330-0
           Ebook   978-1-4836-8331-7

All rights reserved. No part of this book may be reproduced or transmitted in any form or by any means, electronic or mechanical, including photocopying, recording, or by any information storage and retrieval system, without permission in writing from the copyright owner.

This book was printed in the United States of America.

Rev. date: 08/09/2013

To order additional copies of this book, contact:
Xlibris LLC
0-800-056-3182
www.xlibrispublishing.co.uk
Orders@xlibrispublishing.co.uk

INTRODUCTION

TRUE STORY

Henry Joseph O'Prey and Mary Thompson, had been seeing each other for a few months, but had to keep it secret because of religion, Harry, as he was known was catholic and Mary prodestant. Both parents were very strict and devout, but their secret was out and they were about to get the fright of their lives, and would affect both of them, but they didn't know why or what till Harry's ship docked, as he made his way down the gang-plank from the Empress of Canada, looking forward to seeing Mary again, and some leave before his next trip, or so he thought. They would both be twenty one soon, with Harry on the sixteenth of May and Mary the twenty second of June 1947. Harry's ship was at the Albert Docks having just returned from his last voyage from Canada on the Empress of Canada, and there to meet him were his dad and Mary's dad looking like a little Hittler and a face like thunder to match.

They were both looking forward to a double celebration, which they would get, only not the one they were expecting. Mary had been working in a match factory, and Harry was in the Royal Navy. They always met up in the local dance hall and had arranged to meet that night, but Harry and Mary didn't know, that her dad had been keeping her letters, so Harry wasn't prepared for the frosty reception he got the minute he saw both dads, waiting as he came up to the floating bridge. They all got in a taxi, but not one word was said. What's goin on? He asked, but getting just a stare from his dad, which told him not to ask, so nothing was told.

He walked into Mary's home, for the first time ever, as soon as he saw Mary, she was crying in the corner, and sporting a very black eye, but before she could say anything, her father started his tirade, without coming up for air. "What's goin on?" Ill fuckin tell yer what's goin on, yer bleedin Irish get, see that, pointing to a little bundle, thats you're brat, and yer gonna marry that fuckin slut, cos im not having a bastard in my fuckin house, so get the fuckin thing sorted, and quick." As he walked over to see 'the bundle' he picked up his five month old daughter up and he said, 'Why didn't yer tell me Moll? As he called her', but she couldn't get a word in. 'Why? 'So yer could do a fuckin runner, yer wanted a bleedin warnin did yer, well yer gonna marry the bitch, like it or not!. Both parents were shamed, Harry looked at his baby, who was his double with her big mop of red hair. 'Don't worry Moll,' i'll get it sorted. Then off he went, promising Mary he would be back as soon as he got things sorted out.

The first thing he did the next day, was go to his ship, and ask for urgent leave, but was told the earliest he could have was July, so the only date he could get married was on the 2nd August 1947, He was calling himself all the stupid gets under the sun, he wasn't ready for babies, and most of all, he didn't want to get married, but he was left with no choice. Mean-while, Mary had to stay with her sister, Nellie, where Mary had to stay since she found out she was pregnant, and now, she had to go back there until the time she and Harry could marry, the only thing wrong with that, was Nellie lived in Scotland, with her husband Hughie, and two sons Robert and Ian. That meant she wouldn't be able to see Harry, or would Harry get to know his daughter. It was Mary's brother's wife, Norma, who was Franks wife said she could stay with them. Mary's dad couldn't give a shit, as long as she was away from his house.

August was slow coming, but when the time came for Mary and Harry to get married, Mary was over the moon, at least now, their daughter wouldn't have the stigma of being a bastard. Harry was worried about what he was letting himself in for, but the wedding took place, and there was no turning back, he only had himself to blame!

After only four days as husband and wife, Harry would live to regret his actions, he never wanted to marry, and now he felt as though he'd been married for years, not days.

PART ONE

∽

By making a payment of an allottment for her and Teresa, the name they had called their daughter, after only four days, they really didn't come across as only just being married, not when harry couldn't wait to get away from her swearing, and a screaming baby down his bloody ears twenty four hours a bleedin day', Oh god! another hour in there and she would av got the back of my bloody hand, "i can't take much more" . . . . As he walked towards the shipping office, there must be somethin i can do, i can't stay there any longer, he thought Then he saw two of his shipmates, alright 'H' as they called him, hows it goin?, "Don't ask", it's pure hell, i can't even go fer a jar, he told them. When they walked in, they joined the crowd gathered around the notice that had been put on the wall, 'Whats goin on they asked?, they were told their ship was getting checked over, and they wouldn't be sailing, 'Oh Jesus, no! Iv gorra another two days, on his way back to the pub above were they had lived since they got married, and told mary that his ship was leavin in an hour and he had to get packed and quick! He lied to Mary and it was less than an hour, he was gone, leavin five bob on the only chair they possessed. Harry made his way to the seaman's mission by the murky waters of the Mersey, he shoved his bag on a bunk, then with all guilt gone, he headed for the pub for the first pint in ages, he had three pints of bitter, then he started on the rum, he could only manage two tots of rum, then he told his mates he was really tired, then made his way up the scotti road, till he realised he was making his way to where mary was, he turned as soon as he could, before anyone saw him. 'Jesus, that was close, he thought as he headed for the mission, and the first decent sleep since he got married, and sleep he did like a baby.! . . . Harry had only been gone for two weeks, or so mary thought!, as she made her way to shipping office, to collect her first payment from harry's allotment, only to be told there was nothin there and to try again the next day, which didn't please her at all, she stormed out of the office, nearly taken the door with her, "What the bleedin hell am i gonna do with no money?! . . . The five bob harry had left her went nowhere, by the time she payed three bob rent, there was very little left, so off to the pawn shop she went, with harry's suit, the only one he possessed, plus a pair of sheets, which harry's sister gave them as a wedding gift, all neatly wrapped, tessy; now being six months old, she couldn't manage to get far and had to keep stopping, to swap hips, moanin to herself," so called fuckin family, three of them had large prams, only brought out when someone had a baby, the last time one of them was used, was two years ago, but nobody offered to lend her one, the shower of bleeders! . . . She find out?, 'Oh i know where is ship is mrs, but even so, there's nothin er fer yer' im sorry!. 'Sorry won't fuckin feed us,' will it? How come you know where he is?, i don't even know that. 'Aye mrs' it's not my fault yer hubby doesn't keep yer informed, there's no need fer that! Well, yer not doin yer bleedin job then are yer! Where's his ship then, go on tell me, that bastard is gonna get what he deserves, i'll tell yer that for nothin! As it turned out, harry's ship was docked, under goin repairs in Nova Scotia, Canada, and it would take up to two weeks, then carry on with his trip, so god knows when he would get home!; . . . God, 'feel sorry fer the poor sod, whoever he is, comin home to that one!;Harry's trip was goin into two months and mary was beside herself, she had already sold or swapped what bits they had, so she could keep the room on, that harry had found them, although it was now bare it was still a roof over her head, the baby, now coming on to seven months, was getting her dried milk which kept her going for now, even though she should be on solids at her age, mary knew there was nothing she could do!. had taken to robbing milk, sometimes bread, from doorways of pubs in the area, then she and tessy, which she had been called lately, would have warm pobs, which was just warm milk over the bread, to them it was a meal; "If i had my hands round yer fucking neck now yer bastard, i'd fuckin kill yeh, "bet your not goin without a meal or sittin on the bleedin floor freezin are yer!?" . . . . She just sat on the bare mattress, which was her bed and cried! The sound of footsteps on the stairs, told her that may, her landlord was on her way up fer the rent, or so she thought!. After three loud thuds on the door, mary opened the door to see a policeman standin there, the colour must have drained from her face, as she heard the policeman's words, 'don't worry mrs, its nothin bad, can i come in ?,. "Look girl, as he looked around, i know things must be hard fer yer right now, but people av been watching yer, and yer were seen taken stuff off doorsteps, so il just give yer a warnin now, but don't do it again, ok!mary just nodded, her head down, thanks lad, without showin her face, "What next !. she was tired, and hungry, cold and lonely, "don't give a shit any more"! The following day, Mary once again made the journey to the allottmentallot, dreading what she would hear, not wanting to hear the same old girl, nothing again'! but was over the moon to find there was a payment there, and all she had to do, was just sign the book and then she was given the payment; . . . Oh god, her hands shaken as she opened the small bag, she found a ten bob note and two half crowns, she sat down in a corner, and sobbed!, and sobbed!. The man at the desk walked over to her, 'Come on girl, it can't be that bad,' come over here by the stove, 'put the baby by the warm, an il make yer a nice cuppa tea;. After she vented all her past anger for harry, sailor', aye'. "Listen girl, 'have yer been ter the national assistance board'? cos they help people in your shoes yer know', just give them a chance', yer never know!. After agreeing to go the next day, she thanked him again, then made her way to the shop, then suddenly she that six weeks before, that she had been on the housing list and called in before she went back to the pokey room that was her home;! Jesus Christ, 'maybe this was the day, that would change life fer the better, she thought, she had been given the keys to a two bedroom flat! . . . She had to pay five bob rent, and she could move in as soon as she wanted!'The flat was a middle landing of three, and was in a very poor state, but was a palace to what she was in she decided she would move that night!, but how ?. 'Sod it she mumbled to herself', IL sorts it.

PART TWO

∞

On the way back, mary called in the corner shop, which was one of the one's she had taken stuff off its door step, so she felt a bit nervous goin in, but it was gettin late and she needed a few things in hurry, so in she went, most of all some candles and oil for the small oil lamp, which really belonged to the landlady, but mary had other idea's "She can piss off, the fuckin money she's ad off me."! No chance, It was then she planned to do a moonlight flit. The street where she was movin to was Bispham street where she was hoping to get a new start,. Mary thought' but she was in for her biggest shock so far, and just as she was startin to get things together, it couldn't be, wasn't meant to happen, but she remembered that she hadn't had her monthly's. "Oh shit" i can't be, oh, what am i oh god, he's gonna go of his bleedin ed! . . . Mary thought about asking about, but she only knew a couple of women in that area, "She would just wait till after she had sorted out her move, that was the thing she needed to do most! Its probley just late because of all the stress she was under, il be ok when ive settled.

As midnight was getting close, mary was almost ready, having been getting everything she owned, which wasn't much, but she had taken some things that belonged to the landlady of the pub, but the only thing she was worried about, was the mattress that her and tessy had been using was going to be a problem because she had to carry tessy as well! . . . She had been taken bits and bobs down to her new flat when every one's light went out one by one, which would give her the green light to make a move, "Oh shit, she had forgot the two things she needed most of all', the mattress and the oil lamp;" How am i gonna get that,? she pointed to the lump, which was bed to her and tessy.

Mary thought about tessy, then looked at the mattress and wondered, who or what was going first! Tessy or the lump, because she won't be able to carry both . . . . Mary couldn't think what to do, but she had to do something because it was getting late, as luck would have it, tessy was fast asleep at last, so should she chance and take the mattress first and hope that she was back, before tessy hopefully had woken up, so she made her way down the back stairs, when she thought it was safe, she had already rolled the lump up, which was rolled up, so she tied the thing round her back, she slid down or went forward on all fours as quickly as she could,." Jesus, if she woke up, then i will be in the shit!" Luck was on her side, she had made it back, and tessy was none the wiser, so mary wrapped her in an old pink sheet' plus one bag, took one last look at the pit 'and put two fingers up.

Tessy was still asleep, and was still not at aware of what had gone on around her, so Mary made the most of the time, and slept with her. The next day' mary was getting ready to go and see the people that the man at the mission had told her about, To her amazement when they told her to pick whatever she wanted, it was full of stuff that had been donated and was mostly looked new, but wasn't, but to her, it was priceless, so after getting anything she wanted, she was told it would be delivered the next day, she left the hall and set off home . . . smiling all the way. She almost forgot about her other problem, "Jesus Christ, i beta find out where i can get sorted and fast!

The only place she was told about, was the wash house up by ST'Anthony's at the top of the scotti road. From there she had to go to Newham street, only she did'nt know what number house to go to, "oh sod it, she spotted a couple of women on the other corner, il av ter ask them," the two of them told her, 'don't worry girl, she'll sort yer! Don't worry luv, 'We've all been there ourselves!.

After what seemed like a life time, Mary was ready for home, and in a lot of pain, she handed the sixspence over to the women who had solved her problem, and said thanks mrs, and left!

"The pain was tearing her apart, she was still bleeding, but not as bad as she expected "but she had forgotten she had to carry tessy, and as she cringed at every step she called Harry o'prey everything under the sun! It was two months on, when she heard that Harry was coming home, "but not till the week after, "Holy Jesus, that was close" but she was 'not sure why she was still not feeling too well after she had gotten shut of the thing she had aborted, or was it something else, as time would find out! . . . Harry had only a two week pass, up to now, and wasn't too happy going back to mary, but it was a case of having to, "sod it" he said out loud, il tell her i only got a week, and i can stay at the mission for the other week, at least he would have some company there.! Because none of his family wanted anything to do with him, not after the shame he had brought them. Still he thought, she might not be as bad, since getting this new flat she had been going on about! . . . Tessy, now being nearly one and a half years old, would see her dad for the first time since she was only four months old. Mary was still being sick and would have to go the doctor, she didn't want to be like this, As she made her way to the doctor's, she was looking forward to seeing Harry in a way, but she couldn't understand why, after the way he had left her!. But when she came out of the doctor's the smile had gone, from a smile to tears". Mary was told that she was still pregnant, how far gone, she couldn't remember, but the doctor told her that by her dates, her baby would be born sometime in December! 'I can't be, that was sorted, yet as she looked at her belly, she had been conned, by the women that took her money had done a botched up abortion, and she was mortified! . . . but she won't tell Harry till he goes back to sea, but what if should notice, she would have to hope he doesn't . . . As it turned out, he never found out, not yet anyway!!!!!!!!!!

PART THREE

∞

1949

Harry's ship docked finally, the last week in August but before he went 'home', he went the pub with a couple of shipmates, savoring every drop . . . After a few jars, he set off and made his way to the address that mary had sent him, but he was going to tell her that he only had a week, not two" He couldn't spend two weeks with her, by god he couldn't! Number 90 Bispham street, loomed closer to him and he became very uneasy, not like he should be feeling, not at all!. Mary had been making the flat look as homely as she could, and was glad she wasn't showing as much as she thought she would, and wearing a loose frock she had been given, she was happy and looking forward to seeing harry, but more so, seeing his money! "thers no fuckin way im avin another brat, and been left in shit like she was with tessy"! . . . As Harry made his way up the street, he thought he had a welcome home reception, but it was all people from the houses, just having a nose, and natter like normal; and he felt every pair of eyes at the back of his head as he started to climb the stairs, he thought he was headed fer the gallows, not wanting to be there at all! . . . Harry knocked loudly on the front door, and just stood there waiting, when mary rushed into his arms with tears running down her face, albeit crocodile tears 'Oh arry, iv really missed yer", she sobbed, Harry thought as he put his kit bag on the floor, "what the bleedin ell is goin on ere"?. He did'nt expect this, but thought he would make the most of it, as mary pulled him inside. "Are aye girl, yerv'e made it a nice little palace, it's nice an cosey" Av yer been gettin me money ok'?'At first arry, it didn't come through an i ad a horrible time', an as yer know, the bastard's who call themselves fuckin families, they didn't give a fuckin shit!, Harry just nodded as he thought to himself'" See the swearing hasn't got any better"!.' 'Oh don't worry about that lot, we don't need them,' were gonna be ok, at least now we've got a decent place to live,! . . . 'Come on girl, get yerself ready an il take yer fer a jar, completely forgetting about tessy until mary pointed to the bed!' "She'll be ok, she's fast asleep anyway, and we won't be that long and im nackered anyway and the pub's only on the corner, which is handy we'll just av a couple, so hurry up and get yer glad rags on!" Tessy had only just dropped off, so they should be ok if its only fer an hour or so "Mary thought, she'll sleep right through the night now, so they made their way over to the pub, and made themselves at home . . .

The pub was called The Marylbone, and was Billy and Rene Judge, who managed it, introduced themselves to harry and mary, as did a few other regulars, and they all mingled together, having a good old singsong and a few would have a lock in, which included harry and mary, who jumped at the chance to av another few beers; but they lost track of the time, suddenly they both looked at the time, 'Jesus, arry, look at the time' not thinking they had been there over six hours, then they both jumped up and grabbed their coats, it was daylight! They had been there all night, horrified that they had left tessy on her own all night"." Shit arry, i hope she's ok! As they got inside, tessy was screaming, and on the floor, "she looks ok" said harry, "till they found the bed full of shit" all over, plus tessy was full of it as well, but when they looked at tessy's face, they knew that she had been eating it!. 'OH fuck' arry, worra we gonna do?' 'Well im not gonna sleep in it!, he roared, you can do what yer want, just bloody clean her an shut er up, before she wake's the fuckin rest of the street, I've got my kit, il sleep on that till yer clean the bed!' 'Oh, yer all heart yer bastard,' i can see yer avent changed, "na, yer still a selfish bastard, fuck yer,' I've managed on my own up to now, and i can do it now, so yer can fuck off, we don't need yer! . . . Now harry was showing his true colours, 'yer not as saintly as yer mam and dad think yer are, are yeh', . . . 'why the fuckin ell did i marry you?, god knows, if it wasn't fer tessy, yer wouldn't be here,! Mary was nackered by the time she had cleaned the bed, tessy being done earlier, now she had the chore of sorting out tessy and 'the bastard' in the room with something to eat, although there wasn't much to choose from. Harry came out the room, "All right girl" as though nothing had happend, but mary said nothing, "Just keep him sweet just keep him sweet!". While harry slept, mary went through his pocket's and found a lot of loose change, she helped herself to a pound note and ten bob in change, "he won't miss it, i need it more than im". Harry walked over to where mary was, then putting his arms around her, he tried to coach her to go back to bed, but she was having none of it, "I can't arry, im avin me monthly visit", and it normally last's a week, so yer'l av to wait! "Ah aye girl, it's been months, 'and i can't wait that long", I've only got a week! "Thats it' mary thought', thats when i must av been caught with this thing, i fergorra about that and i was still in that pokey room, so the doctor was right, just wait till i get my hands on that stupid cow, when i went to er, i must av been on my monthly then, so she took a tanner off me fer fuck all!, but she won't gerra way with it". Then mary was snapped out of her trance, 'What do yer mean?, yer only got a week, yer told me last night, that yer were home fer two week's! . . .". No, i told yer one, and that i ad ta be back on fer another one before we sailed. Anyway, it's better than a weekend, isn't it? 'And it looks like i picked the wrong week anyway', doesn't it'. he roared, fuck it im goin out! 'He said slamming the door behind him; "yeh, you do that bastard, that's yer answer to everythin, isn't it! And don't fuckin come back, but he did, but this time, mary got what he'd been waitin for! And she felt every blow that was meant for her!" Then without a word, he packed his kit bag and left" and made his way to the mission to finish what was left of his leave, still not aware that mary was pregnant"!

After mary made sure harry's ship had sailed, she decided to go and see her sister in-law, Teresa Robbo, her brother jimmy's wife, They lived in a prefab on Great Homer street, showing two big black eyes, she noticed all the neighbours talkin among themselves, then s she got closer, they would go quiet, there was a gasp when they saw her face, "What the fuck are yer looking at,? Gorra an eyeful did yer"? 'Yer nosey shower of bastard's, Yer not all fuckin snow white yourselves are yer!.

She just pulled a scarf round her face till she got to her brothers "house on bricks as they were known", they looked just like a shed on the outside, but like a normal house inside. When her brother opened the door, 'What the bleedin ell,?' Oh don't worry about that, there's worse to come" "Teresa, his wife was fuming, 'what the fuck as that get done to yer? Come and sit down, she said, taken the little girl from her arms, who was now fast asleep and put her on the bed in the other room, 'Its ok she's fast asleep. Now tell us what's gone on,! Mary started her story, as jimmy and Teresa listened with bated breath, taken everything in, il kill the bastard when i get me hands on him said Jimmy. Mary went to get up, as she heard tessy cry out; don't worry girl, said Teresa, il get her, you stay were yer are, 'Shame, they can't have kids, mary thought, but after five years, they found they never would". "She's a little cracker aint she Jim"? 'Thats why i came to see yer both', then she told them that she hadn't harry about the one she was expecting,' i was too scared to tell him, or he would av bleedin killed me, he was bad enough about tessy" She could see Teresa and jimmy looking at each other, not building her hopes up, but she saw the way they looked, that mary may have the 'problem sorted, her little scheme must be working;! 'Why don't yer stay er the night,? Said her brother!? then we can try helping yer, Its working, mary hoped, i know it is!

Mary told them she wouldn't stay, or rather could'nt she hadn't want to put them out!, anyway,' he's gone back to sea, 'he won't ever lay another bleedin hand on me again;. But she hadn't told them about the abortion she'd had, or that it hadn't worked! . . . 'How far are yeh girl?, 'well the doctor told me, sometime in December, but he couldn't say when, and tessy would be goin on eighteen months when this one arrives!, don't know what im gonna do, 'i, can just about cope with er', pointing to tessy!. Are aye girl, 'yeh must be gettin on now, 'i say yer about six or seven months looking at yer; so yer must be nearly ready by now," yeh, i know, il just av ter tell him, there's nothing else i can do!

'He can't get at me from his ship, can e;'Look girl 'jimmy said, you get yerself home, and come back Tomorrow, in the meantime, me an tre will av a talk then let's see if we can come up with anything, "Have yer got that! So don't worry. As she said goodnight, and closed the door,

Mary walked along scotti road, she smirked, I' know already what yer gonna do, yer pair of stupid gets!

The following morning as mary made her way to jimmy's, she was keeping her head low, she didn't want anyone to see her face, it wasn't that bad last night, as it was dark and there wasn't that many

"Hello girl,' how yer feeling as Mary looked up, she was faced by four women that lived in her street, Mary thought, 'their faces looking really concerned, "and you being in yer condition as well". 'Oh shit, she didn't think she was showin that much', so she must be gettin lose to her time! She just told them she had fell, but she was not too bad, 'sorry, can't stop, im on me way ter doctor's, thanks fer asking, Tara 'Yer never know, they might come in handy one day'mary thought, and at least they seemed ok, but she never heard what they talkin about as they carried on their way!

"She must think were all bleedin stupid, soft cow "no wonder her Fella got off." Little did they know, that by talkin to her, that they would be sorry they openend their mouth!

Just as mary got to her brothers, it was his wife tre who came bouncing to the door, hurry up girl, hurry up, while pulling mary and tessy through the door, "Werv'e yeh been, ? We were startin ta think yer weren't comin! Teresa was dancing up and down, 'ok ok, said Mary, yer look like a bloody jumpin bean, mary sniggered". Look girl, just sit down and listen, we might be able to help yer with yer problem!" Now, befor we get settled, jimmy told tre to put the kettle on, 'then we can explain what we think might be better fer yer, 'Mary couldn't contain herself,' come on lad, what? Just tell me! As yer know, me an tre av been trying fer years to ave kids, but seein you in a state about keepin the one yerv'e gorra birth, "How would yer feel about me an tre having it?, when its born and bring it up as ours?!"an also put it in our name' that way, yer don't av ter worry about the other fella, "But" he should'nt know about it!'Then he said, 'what he doesnt know won't hurt him, meanin harry, he doesn't want another, does he?" . . . . "So, what about that? That way, tre would or, we would rather, have the kid wev'e always wanted. They had played right into Mary's hands just as she planned her twisted little plan had worked"! She put her head in her hands, as though to cry, but they would be happy tears,! . . . "Oh my god lad, i never even gave that a thought, do yer mean that, why did'nt i think?, Then she did start the tears, telling them how close she was gettin an abortion, but it had gone wrong," but are yer sure?, that way were both gettin somethin, and you will get what yerv'e always wanted. "What's happening next? what der yer want me to do, I don't think I've got that long?,' We'll just tell people that we adopted it, so as soon as yer birth it, me and tre will be right there ta take over an take the baby, is that ok with yer"? asked jimmy, 'oh Jim, yer a saint!, and as it happend, two weeks later, they would have their own baby,' Oh mary, yer don't know what this means ter me, sobbed her sister in-law . . . .

PART FOUR

∽

For the following two weeks, mary was worn out, so her sister in-law was never away from mary's though she needed a rest, otherwise she wouldn't be any good ter no one, so she told mary that she needed to go home fer the night, "yer all right fer a while girl" an il be back before yer know it. "but yer can't go now', it could come anytime now the pains are gettin worse, so tre, never got the much needed rest. For the labour had gone on all night, as mary's screams told, it was a bad time, it also told the neighbours, what was goin on.! She didn't think anyone knew about her being pregnant, but she couldn't have been more wrong! Everyone in the scotti road knew, right from the wash house, and the one that was supposed to get shut of it!" Thats what it was like down there, everyone knew everyone else's business ". . . On the twenty second of December, after a long labour, mary gave birth to a baby girl, with jimmy and tre there, looking at the little girl, who was to be their daughter, tre was overjoyed, crying, as jimmy put his arms around her,' oh Jim, look at er, she's ours'". But they wasn't prepared for what came next 'Thats gonna cost yer a fiver!; "What are yeh talkin about? Jimmy said, a fiver?." Well yer didn't think i went through that fer nothin so yer betta make yer mind up, i know someone else who wants 'it' if yeh don't. "Yer 'd sell yer own baby, yer fuckin evil bitch, yer a right bastard,!" Come on tre, before i do somethin il regret, that bitch deserves all she gets! No bleedin wonder none of the street like her', poor tre was brokenhearted, Oh mary, how could yer, how could yer be so heartless,? "Come on girl, she's not worth your tears, jimmy took hold of her and went towards the door, as they got to the door, they heard mary's words," yerv'e got till

23

tomarra "so make yer mind up!;; then jimmy slammed the door behind him.! They both walked home in silence, jimmy fuming, and tre in tears. Jimmy couldn't bear to see his wife so upset', don't worry girl, il sort somethin out! The morning after, jimmy went to see his boss, hoping that he would he out, but he would have to tell him the truth, feeling ashamed that his own sister had done this, but he didn't have to worry, his boss gave him the fiver he needed, then told jimmy to wave it, after he heard what it was for, jimmy was about to say he would pay it back; but his boss just told him to go and save the baby that would certainly have a better life with him and tre!;There were no words to describe the joy, when jimmy said to tree' come on girl, let's go get our daughter,. Jim, that's a bloody week's wage, how? 'How she asked, while pulling her coat on,' ill explain on the way, just hurry up will yer. Jimmy told tre about his boss, she couldn't believe it! Then just as they got to the door', mary was ready and waiting, as soon as they knocked, the door flew open; I' thought yer were 'someone else, "There's yer bleedin money, bitch, jimmy said, telling tre, to pick the box up with the baby,' jimmy asked mary if she had any milk for the baby, not wanting to look at mary," that's gonna cost yer another ten bob; she told him. Fuck! Off, jimmy roared, there's a shop open down by us, we can sort it. That's it! God that Bitch has got a cheek! No wonder know one likes her. Im sorry girl, but if i had stayed a second longer, have done time for that bastard, and she deserves what she gets from the other thing!

They could only manage to get condensed milk for the baby and that would have to do till the morning, which meant tre would have to sort it all out in the morning, because he would be at work, but that didn't bother tre, she was just made up that she had what she had always wanted, such a small thing a baby, which everyone else took for granted, and would always treasure and nothing else mattered.

Jimmy was ashamed that Mary was his sister, how could anyone sell their own baby! But his own sister, he just couldn't see how evil she was, still he thought, but now at least they got her away from the 'thing that called herself a mother. Tre called round to see if Rita would be able to go with her, just to help her carry some thing's for the baby, as soon as she walked in the shop, every stopped talking, being about ten people, some that Mary had told those that had befriended her, that 'She had carried the baby as a favour, for jimmy and tre, but word had soon spread, what exactly had happend, so everyone knew the truth now and by god, Mary would get what was coming to her. At the point tre was going into the shop, she hadn't known that she was the topic of the conversation, until Rita told her that mary's sly trick was all over the streets and by the end of that day everyone would know just how evil, that woman was and is!

Rita and another couple of the girl's that had gone to school with Robbo, as they all grew up together, had all called her, just as a nickname, but it had stuck, so to the name tre was called Robbo. While the shop wasn't too busy, Rita had been very busy, involved with the help of the other two friends, doing what friends do, they stood by Tre all the way, getting stuff together, and by the end of that day, they had collected everything a baby could need right down to a dummy, they armed themselves and made their way towards Great Homer Street feeling right proud of Robbo. As Rita knocked at the door, jimmy stood there, 'what the bloody ell, but before he could finish what he was about to say, they heard Robbo, humming, which brought tears to their eye's, Well, can we come in? Or what, said Rita, only as yer can see, our hands are full, yer daft bugger, get out the way. Robbo fell to her knees when she saw what the girls had brought, 'Oh my god, where as all this come from? Look jimmy, there's everything here from a big pram, sadly only on loan, but all the rest is yours right down to nappy pins Rita was proud to say, and the pram will act as a cot till you can sort one, and the pram is yours, well at least till May, so girl, that should do yer fer a while, and some of the clothes will do fer when she gets a bit older! 'We don't know what ter say girls, we are lost fer words. The look on both yer face's is thanks enough, we are glad we could help, anyway 'have yer thought what yer gonna call her? asked Rita, 'Margaret, after Jimmy's mother, we think she must be a saint to live with that pig. Then they all started laughing. Well, come on you two, I've got a shop to run said Rita, give us a shout if yer need anything else girl and don't forget.

PART FIVE

∞

'That's what the world needs tre, 'Friend's are worth more than any of my family' and yer won't find that anywhere else only in LIVERPOOL, only our friends, we can count on, thats all we need, aye girl! 'Yer right there lad' 'They are worth their weight in gold, that lot! Two weeks later, everyone going about their every day chores, some cleaning windows, others donkey stone on the front doorsteps, when suddenly all activity stopped, to stare at a young woman, riding a bike and trying not to be noticed, which was impossible in Bispham Street, and as she got closer, she knew all eye's gazing at her! So she thought to herself, 'Why is everyone looking at me? Feeling a little scared, she got off the bike and headed for the stairs which led to the first landing, but there was no place to tie her bike to, getting more nervous, till she thought 'sod it', the bloody thing, it will just have to stay there, so as she took out, what looked like a small case and started to go up the stairs.' 'She will get whats coming to her now'. Everyone turned to see who said those words but there was silence among the group, That was till they hear mary's screams 'What the fuck are yer on about?, iv' only got one kid, and there she is. 'So "miss fuckin know all, and tweeds' get down them fuckin stairs before i bleedin throw yer down the lot, the poor girl didn't need telling twice, she really thought mary was going to hit her and she flew down the stairs.! As the young girl made her way down the stairs, almost falling, mary was behind her and then she noticed all the women, Well, i might of known you lot had something to do with this, yer shower of nosey bastards, mind yer own fuckin business, the lot of yer.!As the young girl peddled as fast as she could, too scared to turn around, just kept going until she felt safe and then stopped, just to get herself together.

The following morning, Robbo called into the shop, 'oh girl, yer missed it all yesterday, Rita couldn't get the words out, bloody ell girl, slow down and come up for air will yer, just start again but take yer time!..

Bloody ell, it doesn't take long fer the jungle drum's round here doe's it" Anyway, girl, will yer just put this in yer window fer me, it's only a note to thank everyone fer what they done. Arh aye girl, you don't have to, you and jimmy have give that baby a better life, better than that one, the baby is better off away from her, yer were that baby's way out, so give yer self a pat on the back!.

It was a week later, before Mary showed her face, but she wasn't gone long before she came back, covered in rotten eggs, among other things including threat's!. 'Jesus Christ, what am i gonna do now? I need ta get down the shipping office, but how can i with that fuckin lot! "You fuckin bastard, Harry O'prey, you bastard. Every fuckin time yer come home, i always end up fuckin pregnant, and you are never around when yer needed" she screamed at the broken piece of mirror that hung on the wall. She was covered in rotten eggs and dog shit, mingled with tears. Mary didn't expect Harry home for about four weeks, but what she didn't know, was that Harry had already docked the night before, "and had gone to the Grapes pub on the scotti road, but as soon as he walked through the door, he could feel the tension, as many pairs of eyes glared toward him, he got a very frosty reception." What the bloody ell is goin on? 'Come on, will someone at least tell me? Fer God sake, the landlord looked at Harry, thinking, the poor sod don't even know' so he pulled Harry to one side and told him everything that had happend. Harry felt the blood rushing to his head, and drain from his face, as the landlord handed him a large glass of rum, Sorry lad, we thought yer might av already been told.

As soon as Harry heard the story, he left his pint, but he downed the whiskey the landlord had gave him, 'Im gonna need this', he told him. Then, he bolted as fast as he could and made his way down to his brother-law's, without a backward glance, not even thinking of Mary. As he got closer, his rage was beginning to rise, so he stood inside a shop doorway to have a much needed cigarette, he needed to calm down.

As soon as Harry knocked on jimmy's door, he was set on by jimmy, not expecting this, 'Harry bit back, aye hang on, at least tell me whats gone on,' because i know fuck all.! 'We know that yer didn't want little Margaret, who by the way is goin on six months old now, just take a look at what yer bleedin wife "Sold us" yeh, you heard right, 'Im even ashamed to call her a sister, cos there's a few other word's i could call er' It shocked Harry to the core, to think anyone could sell their own baby, never mind his own wife, the evil bitch! Robbo looked as the colour left Harry's face, and she really felt sorry for him. 'She knew by the look on Harry's face that he didn't know anything about it. 'Sit down lad' the kettle's just boiled, a cup of strong tea and plenty of sugar, cos yer need one by the look of yer, so while she was sorting the tea out, jimmy told Harry the whole story, much to his disgust, he sat and took on board every word jimmy was telling him, trying hard to control his temper.!

Harry looked at the little girl, and thought she was the image of her mother, even he felt sorry for her, having that evil bitch fer a mother, he also knew she would be better off with jimmy and tre. Jimmy could see what was going on in Harry's mind, he knew what he was thinking, 'Don't even think about it "mate" she's in our name, and we've got a lot of good friends,' anyway, you an er don't deserve kids, so now yer can fuck off out of my house and don't show yer face er again!. Harry made his way back to the mission, he didn't want to see Mary, if he did, he would do something he would regret, and after what he had just heard, she wasn't worth it.

Harry made the journey to the mission, his head in his hand' not knowing what to do next, but it would be sorted, he'd make sure of that! Something was gonna happen, jimmy thought, he knew it was because he knew Harry wasn't the type to let things go so easy, but right now, he was worried about his wife and how happy she had been the last six months, and little Margaret, what would happen to her, he dreaded to think. Little did they know, that their worst fear's where about to come true, but not even knowing that the heartbreak that was coming, would be the break up their little family, and the suffering they would endure.

The lady who had been scared to death of Mary, was about to pay Mary another visit, but this time she would have company in the form of a policeman and Harry! The same person had known that Mary's husband was a seaman, was waiting in the mission, when someone told her that the bloke she had been waiting for, meaning Harry had just walked in. She had sat there for what seemed a lifetime, she got up and asked Harry could she have a word, 'I think i know what this is about luv, but can we talk somewhere private away from here.

After a long conversation, they both made their way to the police station, then from there, they headed back to jimmy's in silence, but Harry knew what the outcome would be.! Four loud bangs on the door, making jimmy and Robbo jump, now with the added cries of the baby being woken up, 'who's that at this hour? Remarked jimmy, as he opened the door, jimmy came face to face with Harry and the policeman plus the lady from the social service office. For two hours, there had been a lot of talking, and agony for poor Robbo who was in tears as they were told they had to give the baby back. "You bastard" Why? Look at my mrs, her heart is breaking, but you don't give a shit about that, do yer, my dad was right about you, i hope yer can live with yerself, yeh piece of shit. Poor sods, thought the policeman, this poor kid is not gonna get the love and care where she's going back to. Its times like this that he didn't like his job, as he handed the baby to the woman from social worker, who would then look after her overnight. Robbo just crumbled to the floor, and sobbed her heart out, jimmy could do nothing except hold her till his tears mingled with her.

PART SIX

~~

Now, Mary and Harry had been ordered to the to the police station, and only now did Mary find out that Harry was already home, and this was the first time they came face to face, as Harry had not been home and when she saw the anger in his face scared her,! "What's goin on? She asked, thinking Harry had done something wrong,"

When the story started to unfold, Mary went into action, 'I tried to get shut of it arry, i really did, then i was told i was too far gone. "It was then our jimmy asked if him and his mrs could have 'it', as she couldn't even say daughter, anyway, you where not supposed to know, 'yer didn't want 'it' anyway so why all the bleedin fuss now'. 'It's because you sold your own fuckin baby,' yer fuckin evil bitch', 'Oh don't worry, i know all about it, the whole of scotti road knows, 'Why the fuck do yer think i didn't come home the last two nights, yer make me fuckin sick. That day was the beginning of little Margaret's downfall, by the hand of a mother who didn't want her, and made sure that she would pay the price, just for being born!

It was 1952, and Mary was to find herself pregnant, which didn't seem to bother her, 'Oh fuck, not again, having been to the Sixpence woman after Harry's last trip. Tessy was now five, and at school, and Margaret was due to start in the infants, but both being in the same school, but most of the time, they didn't go anyway, Mary alway's kept tessy home which didn't please tessy,' Why can't she do it?' pointing to Margaret, 'Oh don't worry about her, there's plenty fer that "thing" to do, but i like school, mam said tessy, 'Don't fuckin argue, yer not goin, and that's final! Tessy just puffed and went to put her pump's away, giving Margaret a sly punch as she passed, i hate you! Why did yer av ter come back here? they should av kept yer at that place, After what had happend, Margaret was taken into a children's home for a while, only being allowed three days a week, for a few month's till Mary was allowed to have her back, even though she still didn't want her, she just wanted the extra money she would get. As Mary was still under scrutiny by any and everyone that knew her, she had to "put on a show" just for them, but they didn't see what went on behind closed doors. Mary would have to watch her back, as nobody never forgave her, after what she did to poor jimmy and Robbo, above all, how did she manage to get the little girl back, they fumed. NOW MARGARET TELLS HER STORY . . . .

THE LEAVING OF LIVERPOOL

A SURVIVOURS STORY

PART ONE

∞

MY MAM AND DAD! "That's a laugh". If i had been older, and had understood what had gone on, I would never have called them Parent's, not by my standard anyway, they were far from it.

As i have told my own kid's, i live in the past, not the present, because my past will haunt me for the rest of my life. At the age of four, when i should have been in school, or rather the infant's but, as usual, mother didn't give a shit, as long as i didn't get under her feet, God forbid. I was just told to get out and stay out, so i just had to amuse my-self, till i was allowed back in, so it was no wonder i always landed my-self in trouble?

I go back as far as from the age of three when we lived in Bispham Street, just off the infamous Scotland Road, there was only myself and Teresa, with only eighteen months between us, then in 1952, we were joined by little Harry, a chip off the old block, and the apple of his mother's eye, It seemed every time dad was on leave, Mother was left pregnant, but a visit to "the baby doctor" seemed to fix her problem, but this time again, she was too far gone, then when she had a little boy, she was over the bloody moon, and couldn't wait to tell dad, 'surely he would want a son, thought mary! Dad was happy, but tessy wasn't, she didn't like anyone who got more attention than her, even me, but i already knew that, but couldn't understand why, because i got sod all anyway, and if i did, it was only her hand me down's. Because now there were three kids, Mother, had gone to the housing office to ask for a bigger place, because the flat we in was already too small, and when father was home on leave, we would all have to sleep in the one room, while mother and father slept in the living room, and woe betide anyone who made a noise, when they had been to the local pub on the corner! After 'he' had gone back to sea, mother was told that if she had gone to the corporation a week earlier, she could have had the two bedroom flat two doors away from us, but it was gone now, she was told. How come it's empty? There's curtain's up and she would have known if anyone had moved'. The cheeky bastard, telling me i should get out more, she said to herself, but that was near or there, she had been afraid to go out on her own, since what happend to her brother and sister in-law, my uncle jimmy and his wife teresa, or 'Robbo' as everyone called her, because there were too many Teresa's in both sides of the families, it just made things' more simple for everyone one else, but she had been given the nickname at school, and it stuck and for some reason 'mother' was afraid to go out, if she didn't want to, then she wouldn't bother, but if she needed too, then she would keep me and teresa,' beg your pardon, 'tessy' as she was called then, and that was only when 'mother was in a good mood, which wasn't very often since 'little harry' had been born, which meant tessy was no longer the little goody two shoe's that she used to be, but she still got up to her sly tricks, one's for which only i would suffer from. A week later, we were to find out who had been given the flat that mother went after, and should have been my mother's, She was, for want of another word, Gobsmacked. It was my lovely aunty tre and uncle jimmy! My mother had a face like a smacked arse, and i was over the moon!

The day i started school, i was petrified because everybody just stood in groups, in which tessy was one of them and she told them all to ignore me, she even pretended not to know me, and it was later that first day, that i was to find out why! I ran out of that school as fast as my skinny legs let me and declared that no way, i was going back there. I didn't go home, because i would end up black and blue, so i made my way down to the scotti, as it was known then, i used to make for the big shop on the corner, it kept me amused for ages, most of all the big prams, i had Always wanted one of those, i dreamed of one, but like everything else, it was only a dream.

I was snapped out of my daydream by a big hand on my shoulder, which scared the life out of me, but i needn't have worried, it was my lovely aunty tre, the one person who cared about me . . . She asked me why i wasn't in school, and was fuming when i told her why! 'Come on, she said, taken my hand, 'let's sort that little madam out!

But after she saw the way i was dressed, she changed her mind, 'let's do a bit of shopping first, aye girl, yer not going ter school like that', with that we went down to the market on Great Homer street,' don't worry about yer bloody mother' il sort her out,' Fancy sending yer ter school like that!. Come on, let's get yer somethin to eat first aye, what did you have fer yer breakfast this morning? 'Nothin i said, there was nothin.

After we had a big meat pie, and gravy which i could have eat all over again, we went shopping and i was amazed at the stuff that some of the people gave aunty tre, without charge, and other's only charging copper's, she then took me to the public bath's where i had a nice hot bath, which i had never had before, with the added bonus of lovely smelly soap, she then started to throw everything that she had to more or less, scrape off me and put them in a bag, which she intended to hit my mother with, but i knew she wouldn't, because it would be me that would suffer, she promised she wouldn't when i started to cry,! After she had sorted me out, i looked like a different girl, then i looked at what i had been sent to school in, that's when i knew the kids at school acted the way they did. Everybody had been told to stay away from me because of the way i looked and not because of who i was . . .

When i was all done and dusted, as they say! My mind went back to why other kid's were not allowed to go near me, i cringed, I had dirty clothes on which tessy had already worn for three days before me, my pumps were about two sizes too big, no socks or under wear on, i was never allowed that Privilege, the pumps came from the chute, which was the bin on the landing, which everybody had to share, there were no toes in the pumps and pieces of cardboard inside because they had no soles. When my aunty tre took me back to school, i cried, 'i don't want to go back there, i begged, please don't take me back. Aunty Tre told me everything would be ok now. As we went toward the gates, we were met by a young looking lady, who told us that her name was Miss Scott and she was to be my teacher, she seemed nice enough so aunty tre took her to one side, just so i wouldn't overhear what they were talkin about, i could just see heads nodding, and next thing, she came and took my hand, aunty tre gave me a kiss on the cheek, as she told me everything was ok now, and she would meet me when it was home time. 'Go on girl, It's ok now.' The school was called Holy Cross, and was just at the bottom of the street we lived in, but it could have been the gallows for all i cared, and started to cry after my aunty, but when i turned round, she was gone. "I had just wet my knickers without being aware of it, because i'd not been used to wearing them," my lovely new knickers, i bawled my eyes out. "I want ter go home, i told Miss Scott, i don't like it here, let me go home, wetting myself again. That was my first day at school, a day i will never forget.

My first day was strange to say the least, my teacher took me to a large room, but not a classroom, she told me it was a storeroom, i was none the wiser, but i did know it was bigger than the bedroom that me and tessy slept in. She came out of the room carrying a large box, which she proceeded to empty onto the big table that was in the corner and i stared in wonder. 'Come over here, she told me', she must have noticed how scared i was, so she came to me and walked me over to the table and sat me down, then realised my knickers were wet, so she took me to the toilets, bringing a few items with her.' Just take them off and give yourself a little wipe, she said, handing me a wet flannel and a snow white towel. After she had gave me clean under clothes to put on, we then went back to the table, where she carried on where she had left off, sorting all kinds of everything, from knickers and socks, right up to coats, dress's and shoes, i couldn't take it all in, it was like going to a grotto for the first time, not that i knew what a grotto was anyway, at that time. By the time she had finished, it was dinner time tell you what Margaret, 'why don't you and me have our dinner together? Just us two, we can sit in here, how about that?. 'I don't have any money miss, i said, 'Oh don't you worry your lovely little head about that' she said. I looked around to see who she was talking to, but there was no-one there. I had never been used to any-one talking like that to me before, except my aunty tre. 'Let's go and see whats for dinner shall we'.

The first school dinner i ever had, it was a big plate full of stew and dumplings, I could only have dreamt about, plus a pudding of creamy and soft rice made from real milk, i thought i had died and gone to heaven, My so-called mother would have made just the dinner last a week, never mind rice pudding, and when i found out that i would be getting a free dinner and pudding every day at school, no-one could keep me away, the only downfall about that was i wouldn't get nothing for tea off mother, tessy did, but it didn't bother me, i always had the next day to look forward too. The parcel of clothes i was given by My teacher, was quickly snatched out of my hands, before being told politely to 'Fuck Off" and get to bed'. I wasn't bothered, still being full up by the dinner at school, it was only being told the following morning that i wasn't going to school, i was gutted, but i need not have worried, my guardian angel said she wouldn't let me down, and she never did. That was two i had, so was i bothered, in "mother's slang," was i fuck! But i was going to need my angel's, i just didn't know when, but i was soon to find out. 'Where the fuckin ell did yer get these from? She pointed to the clothes, dragging me by the hair off the bed, slapping me across the face till it was swollen, i told her, aunty tre bought me some and my teacher gave me the bag, i spat the words out, followed by the blood caused by the constant slapping, Thats why i was kept home from school! The following day, my face was so sore as was every part of my body, because she had really been pissed off, mainly because aunty tre had 'stuck her fuckin' nose in as she put it. "Your' not avin these," they will look better on tessy,

PART TWO

~

When tessy had gone to school the next day, Miss Scott asked her why i wasn't in, while noticing the clothes she had on, tessy had told her she didn't know why, after being warned by 'mother' to keep her gob shut, but she didn't give a shit anyway, why should she.? At dinner time, there was a knock on the door, 'See who that is you' meaning me, but i was that sore, i had to move slowly, and because of that i got another punch in the face, knocking two front teeth out. Whoever it was must have heard my scream, and the knock's got louder and longer, until there was shouting through the letterbox, then she really kicked off and opened the door her-self, and she wasn't too pleased when she saw who it was! Miss Scott was stood there, none too happy about kept waiting, but when she saw the state i was in, she demanded to know how i had gotten the injury's i had, and threatening to get the police unless 'mother' told her. After being told a cock and bull story, Miss Scott wasn't fooled one bit. "That woman is dangerous", she thought, but she wouldn't just let it go, 'been fighting' 'she must think i am stupid, but she was worried about me, and she would have to do something about it, "I couldn't live

After a week to recover, and a warning from Miss Scott about the clothes she expected to see me in, i was allowed back to school and i was over the moon, but still a bit worried about the other kids, i was approached by a girl who lived across the road from me, Maggie O'Neil, one of the kids who had been told not to play with me, before my transformation, now wanted to be my friend, then one by one, more of the other kids came over, wanting to be my friend, much to tessy's dismay, i finally relaxed, and couldn't have been happier.

"Where did yer get them nice clothes"? Even some of the mother's, who had brought their kids to school had to look twice at me, 'It was Miss Scott who gave me them" i told them, watching Maggie's face moving up and down my body, 'Oh, so yer the Teachers pet now are yer! 'It's not my fault i said, i didn't know she was gonna give me them'. 'Come on then' said tessy, just leave er, lets finish our game', No they said, we are gonna play with Margaret now, 'I bleedin hate you,' just wait till we get home, yer little shit.' Giving me a sly kick as she walked away! Tessy was home before me, so i didn't know what she had told 'mother', so i just walked in as normal, when i was told to get straight to bed, with a half cup of water, and if i was lucky, a dripping butty where as tessy had the luxury of warm milky tea and a sugar butty, sniggering as i went toward the room.

It was two weeks after my 'injury's by 'fighting' episode, I was lying on the make shift bed in the corner of the room, it was made from flock, and had been thrown out by someone, and it was filthy and all i had over me, was bits of paper and an old coat, that was the only thing to keep me warm, there was a knock at the door, it must have been late, because 'mother' had taking to having a couple of bottles of ale at night, sitting by the fire, so close that she got pock marks on her legs,' Who the bleedin ell is that at this hour', Un be known to me, my teacher had kept to her word about looking after me, she had been to see my aunty tre, and told her everything about the way she had found me on that day of her visit, little harry was fast asleep, well he was, until 'mother' started ranting,. 'What the fuckin ell do you want? Then i heard my aunty tre' 'I want ter talk ter, just hear me out, then il go'. Tessy and me, should have been asleep, but we were sat on the floor by the door, we couldn't really hear all the conversation, just a few snatched word's, but they were talking for age's, but 'mother never spoke, which was strange, we got so tired, we just fell asleep, not even hearing the front door close. The following day, we all got a surprise, 'Father' came home on leave, without any warning, 'Mother hoped he wouldn't notice the state the place was in, but she needn't have bothered, all he was interested in was his precious son, he was over the moon, even tessy was treated the same as me, which she didn't like, i was glad, now she knew how i felt. 'Come on Moll', as he called her', we can just make the last hour, 'What about little Harry,' she said' 'As he been fed? 'Yeh she said. 'We then, these two can watch him for an hour, he's fast asleep anyway'. 'Mother didn't need telling twice, taking all of five minutes, then they were gone. I can't to this day, call them 'mum' and 'dad' because to me, they never treated me like a daughter, there was no love for me, so why should i love them,? I never knew what love was, but i know i was cared for by my aunty tre, and wondered why i was taken away from her, when i wasn't wanted anyway! After they had been gone about ten minutes, tessy pushed me out of the front door, telling me to get lost and wouldn't let me back in. It was very dark, and i couldn't get any answer at aunty Tre's and was starting to get scared until i heard noises down in the street, so i went to see who it was, It was Maggie O'Neal and a few other kids, i thought about going down to join them, but i was more scared of what tessy would tell my 'parent's, but knowing she would come up with something that would get me in trouble anyway, i went down to play with the other kid's. They had a big rope tied to a lamp post, and made a swing out of it, it was great, worth getting a belt for, because that's what would happen, but i didn't care.

One by one, the other kids were called in by their mum, taking the rope with them, leaving just me and Maggie to twiddle our thumb's, so we decided to go for a walk and headed for the scotti, we knew it would be light, because of the amount of pubs that where open, plus the hustle and bustle of people around the area.

The lights and music coming from the pubs was brilliant, there were people all hanging outside of the pubs, a few of them giving us a few copper's, even a sixpence sometimes, we were made up, the first place we made for was the chip shop and Maggie said 'let's get scallops, 'What's them,? I had never had them before, slices of potato and batter never tasted so good, then a fishcake after, The best meal ever. We started to make our way back towards home, till we got lost that is, then we heard someone shout us, though not by name, this was an old man across the road, then before i had a chance to say anything, Maggie grabbed my hand and flew across the road and i had never been scared as i was then.' Come on', he'll help us, so we just went up to him, he gave me a pack of crisp and i looked around to give Maggie some, but she was no-were to be seen, she'd gone and left me, and i started crying. The next thing i know, this old man took me down an entry then i was pushed up to a wall, his hand pulling my knickers down and i felt his hand touch me, in the place that i peed from, i started to cry, when a policeman spotted me, i didn't know if i should be scared of him or glad to see him.

The policeman could clearly see i was upset, he just leaned over me, looking like a giant, and took my hand. I knew i was sitting in a big chair, for a short time and the policeman was asking me questions while he was writing things in a little book, which seemed to be hours, when another policeman came in with my so-called parents, whose faces were like thunder. After that, i was to find out when i was older, by my aunty tre, that they had been told to return to the police station, and were charged with leaving minor's underage, though they tried to con the police by saying they had left us with a babysitter, but the police were not having any of it, they were also told if it happend again, they would suffer a lot more, they were warned.! With a promise of a weekly visit from the children's department of the social workers, which didn't make mother very happy, 'Won't be able ter bleeding fart around here', thanks to that little shit', i gather she meant me. She called father, every word under the sun, again. After word had got round about me and what had happend, he soon scarped back to his ship, although he wasn't due back, he wasn't going to hang around here, so he upped and left mother to face it on her own.

PART THREE

∞

It was six weeks later, when i was to find out about the conversation that had taken place with my aunty tre and mother, which i had completely forgot about since when i was molested, but i had noticed that mother was being very fishy with aunty tre, but i thought nothing of it, so when mother told tessy to watch little harry, while she went to see Robbo, as she still called her, my ears pricked up 'Has mother been talking to aunty tre,? i asked tessy, 'I don't bleedin know, ask her yerself, She was so full of herself was tessy, now being six and a half.

From what i found out later that night, my aunty tre had asked if she could have me stay with her, and she would pay mother two shilling a week!" My mother agreed to this on one condition", that i would have to be back' if and when father was home on leave, to which aunty tre agreed and also, he mustn't know about the money.

I was dancing all over the place when i heard this, i couldn't believe it. It was only two hours later, when mother told me to get my stuff together, i thought what stuff, i had nothing, only the clothes i stood up in, but i wasn't going to let that spoil things for me, so when aunty tre came to 'collect' me, she told me not to worry about clothes, she had it sorted, i just ran towards the open arms, where i had always wanted to be, back with my lovely aunty tre!. I didn't think i could be any happier. I was being 'sold' again, but i didn't care, i was too happy to care and nothing would change that, 'Come on girl, told yer i wouldn't let yer down, didn't i?, she said, and if mother heard them words, then she really didn't care about me, this proved it, she never even bothered to turn, but my happiness was shortlived, as i was to find out later.

NO, NO, im not goin, i want to stay here, please aunty tre, don't let them take me, don't, i pleaded, but to no avail. But this time, aunty tre couldn't do anything about it, though she reassured me it wouldn't be for long, but after so many promises, it was tearing me apart! I felt let down and unwanted again, it had been so often, i got to the stage where i couldn't trust anyone. The reason i had to leave aunty tre, was that we had to move, somewhere called Kirkby, way out of Liverpool, no-one had heard of it, someone said it was out in the wilderness, and we weren't the only ones having to move, most of the street were going, so it wasn't just us, some-one said they were knocking the street down and everyone would be moving, but not all to the same place. It was coming toward the end of 1952 when we moved to Kirkby, we had a maisonette on the ground floor, It had a big front garden, and a even bigger one at the back, three big bedrooms with stairs leading up to them, an inside toilet, and a bathroom with a real bath, but the one thing that made everybody happy was the electric lights, in every room. There came one more time, before we left Liverpool for a weekend leave, before Father had to go back to sea, so mother had to make the most of him, because he said this time, he didn't know how long he would be gone this time. We arrived in Kirkby, in the early hours of the morning while other people slept, he finished work at the market, which fitted in nicely with mother's plan, which was to do a moon-light flit' because she owed certain people money, so the less anyone knew, the better, but before we got there, father dropped his bombshell,'. 'I won't be coming with yer girl,"I heard from the lads, that every-one has been called back early to get ready for sailin. He wasn't ready for what came next.

"And what the fuckin hell am i supposed to do with this fuckin lot? "With three fuckin kids round me neck and him only one year old! She said, pointing to harry junior. 'Im sorry moll, you will just have to get on with it, if i don't go, there won't be any money, and they will only send the police after me anyway! He gave mother what money he had then he was gone, again. "The bastard', he could'nt fuckin wait" she said out loud. She was right.

Christmas came and went, just another day to us, because we didn't know any different anyway. Tessy was six and a half and i was just five, and little harry was coming on for three months old. Many weeks had passed, before mother had any money from father's allottment, plus she discovered that she was also pregnant again, but she hadn't seem that bothered, not like she had in the past. We had been in Kirkby or rather an estate in Kirkby, called West-Vale, number 49 Stanton Crescent, sounded posh, compared to scotti road.

IT was a few months after we moved there, before school was even thought about, we thought it was because mother was to drop another "Brat" as we were called then. It was only when a knock at the door changed that. Tessy was ordered to answer, being told by mother to say she wasn't in, but before tessy got a word out, the voice shouted "Get your body out here Mrs, Now. Tessy had run in, being scared by the man that stood there, who was a priest, mother came to the door, wringing her hands, something she did when she was nervous.

"WHY are these children not attending school?" he introduced himself as Father Murphy, 'I was going tomorrow she lied, to see when they can start, 'They start tomorrow morning, the summer break is over so they begin a new term! After a few words with mother, he said before he left, 'Make sure they have their pennies for the church'. Cheeky bastard, said mother, mocking the cloth he wore. 'Well, that's that, you two, meaning me and tessy, get up them stair's and sort out something to wear, then get washed and ready fer bed. I was in for the shock of my life, but didn't know it then.

We went to the school on our own, mother couldn't be arsed moving her legs away from the fire, all her legs burning, full of pockmarks, nothing new. We had to report to the headmaster's room, until our teacher's came to collect us,. When tessy had gone, i thought i was forgotten about, then when my teacher came, i screamed with delight, It was only my guardian angel, Miss Scott from Holy Cross, i was over the moon, and she gave me a little wink as she took my hand.! Mother was to hear that the government had brought out something called Family Allowance, which meant that mother could get extra money for the kids, but not the eldest, but for me and harry, very soon to be joined by another 'brat'. I remember mother's sister, Margaret, surprise, surprise, was in her element, someone to clean the place,. It was while auntie Margaret, was there, that mother went into labour, with the other brat, she gave birth to yet another girl, whom she named Ann Patrica, but at least she would get extra money as well for this one, that's all she cared about, Money, Money. This was to be proved some years later, Tessy was kept at home to help with the brood, while harry and my-self were dragged from bed to go and find work, 'What planet was she on? We should have been in school, but she had heard from one of her so-called friend's told her that she should send us 'spud' picking, at the farm's in Maghull, we had never heard of it. But before she had a chance to send us, father came home without warning, it was little harry who sounded the alarm, 'It's Me dad, it's Me dad, he shouted, running toward him, arm's out ready to be put on his dad's shoulder. That put mother's plan out of action, for a while anyway! The school was getting on at mother, because of our attendance, which didn't please father, so he put his foot down, he also told aunty Margaret to leave as well, which mother wasn't happy about, but kept her mouth shut. He was different, somehow, but mother couldn't put her finger it, so she kept her mouth shut, 'What's this then? Another girl, pointing to Ann, he completely ignored me and tessy. 'Where's the nearest pub moll? 'There's no pub, only a social club, called Holy Angel's mother told him,' it's next to the school these go to, meaning me and tessy, she had little harry and the latest arrival Ann. It seemed strange the way they argued all the time, when they were in the house, and two completely two different people when they were at the club, which was nearly all the time, while he was home, also he had taking to knocking mother about. While father was home, we were ordered to bed at five thirty every night, no matter what the weather was like, for instance summer-time, it wouldn't go dark till about ten, but come five thirty, bed he ordered, and if we made the slightest sound, he came thundering up the stairs, the buckle of the belt came toward us, me mainly, because mother would shield tessy with her own body, she never gave a shit about the rest of us, well mabe little harry, just!!!!!!!!.

Because as you would expect, we didn't know father that well because he was never home, 'What had we done'? We got to the stage when we didn't like him and started to defy him, well me and harry did, tessy was up his arse, Yes dad, No dad, would tell him anything that would get me a good belting, how i hated her then. 'Come on moll, let's get ready and go to Holy Ash-bag's, his name for Holy angel's, telling 'Teresa' as she was to be called then, 'make sure them little bleeder's stay in bed or they'll answer to me." He warned! "And he had the nerve to order us to church every Sunday", he'd also find out if we didn't go via Father Murphy. By the time he did go back to sea, me and harry hated him, plus we had to stay off school till the weal marks from the time's we had been on the other end of his belt, but being glad to see the back of him made us a lot happier. Then mother started again with her plan, we thought she had forgotten about, but clearly didn't, she dragged me and harry out of bed at six o'clock, she was told about a farm that needed pickers. We were given a cup of hot chocolate and some toast by the farmer's wife, the toast being like doorsteps was gone in five minutes, as was the hot drink. We had to work for ten hours and then make our way to the back door, where there would be sacks of spud's and other stuff including some fruit, to which the farmer told everyone to take what we could carry, me and harry looked at each other, thinking we weren't expecting this, we thought we would get money, but our fear's were put at rest, when the farmer put two half crown's in both our hands, "five bob" "each", we had never seen that much money, come to that, we had never seen a half crown before. "Harry spoke first, 'Shall we give 'her' all this he said? We done all the bleedin work, so why should she have it all? 'Fuck her', we'll keep one each, 'she won't know, and she's got all this as well, but these, we can have on our way home, two massive oranges which were called 'Jaffa's.

Mother was made up with what we took home, then her face was brighter still, when we both gave her the money, "bleedin ell" she said, yer can go again tomarra! 'Oh aye mam, do we have to, its bleeding miles away' harry said, not realizing he had swore, and mother never heard, so he got away with it that time. She told us to sit at the old table, which she had been given by a neighbour, we thought we were gonna get something to eat, and wait while she counted the money, then to our horror, she told us to take our clothes and shoes off, we were both terrified in case she was gettin the belt out, but she just checked to make sure we had gave her everthing, the bitch, she never even offered us a penny, but then again we never expected her to, we knew she wouldn't so it was just as well we had hid the money that we did keep, we went upstairs to bed sniggerin.

PART FOUR

～

It seemed to go on forever this spud picking, with me and harry, sometimes we would not go, then we used to go down the river Holt, and mess about in the tunnel's then go home when we were hungry, telling her there was no work but she was never satisfied, 'Then go to another farm", it didn't worry her how far we had to walk, or how tired we got, all she cared about was the bleedin money, we could break our backs every day for all she cared. We both agreed that we wouldn't go anymore, no matter what she said or did, we wanted to go back to school, that was till we were told that she had told the school that we had gone to live with my uncle George, in Birmingham, so we were not even on the register at the school!. But that changed in the week to follow, when mother was charged and fined with shop-lifting from the local arcade. It was also reported in the Liverpool Echo. Next thing we knew, father was home again, not to happy to see mother's name in the paper. That same night, we all heard mother screaming at father to leave her alone, till he finally fell asleep in a drunken state, the state of mother's face the morning after, told its own story, and for the first time ever, i felt really sorry for her.

1961, brought another addition to the family, another girl who was called Caroline, and the last baby to be born to Harry and Mary O 'Prey, though in the coming years, i was to learn that there had been eleven pregnancy's, but only five had lived. It was when Carol, as we then called her, was eight months old, she was rushed into hospital, and was close to death with Meningitis, caught from a rabbit that harry kept hidden in the airing cupboard, but the hospital saved her. There seemed no end to the problems that cursed this family, and it still wasn't over yet. We got home from school one day, and there sat at the table, was someone i would know backwards, looked at me and held her arms out to me, but i held back, till i realised who it was, then i ran like dust, it was my lovely aunty tre, but why was she here,? Mother was talking as though nothing had happend, you're in the mood fer some good news, then il tell yer some, thats if yer want ter know she said, 'Me and uncle jimmy are moving up here', well not far from here,' its called South-dean, just up the road, so Margaret, do yer want ter come and help me, cos uncle jimmy's got work, and i can't do it all on my own! I jumped at the chance, then looking at mother, just in case i was counting my chickens sort of, but she said ok, but only till Sunday, school Monday, don't forget. It seemed to be spreading, this family all moved to Kirkby, after my aunty tre, came Aunty Nelly, who i had never met, i remember mother saying she lived in Aberdeen Scotland, but aunty tre had told mother that her husband, Hugh, had died so she moved back here with her two son's Robert and Ian Wilson their names were. Everyone was moving to Kirkby, while unbeknown to us, we were about to find out we would be leaving, but we were the last to know!

Me and a few girl's i had gotten to know from school, now at the age of twelve and a half, i was in senior school, called ST Gregory's which i did'nt like, they would give you the cane, if you were as much as five minutes late and it bleedin hurt, it got you right on the tips of your finger's it smarted all day. Teresa had been told she could leave school if she could find a job to help support the family and she wasted no time getting it.

She had got a job in a big shop, now known as a super market, it was called Tesco and was only down the end of the road and mother shrieked 'Well done girl, i knew you would do it'. 'Oh mother was over the moon, her daughter had a job, so what, she wasn't the fuckin Prime Minister, Jesus all that just because she got a job. It wasn't long before father was home again, but mother wasn't too happy, not since he had taken to knocking her about, it took a while for her to heal from the last lot of bruise's he gave her. He didn't take any notice of 'the latest addition to the family Carol at first, it was only when mother asked him for more money, he lashed out. 'Is that all you fuckin care about,? Fuckin money, we knew what was coming next,' Get out and play you lot, and don't fuckin come back in till i say so' Teresa was at work, so me, harry, and Ann didn't get called back in for two hours, a cup of water, and a jam butty before being sent to bed, if we were lucky that is. Father then told mother that his time in the Royal Navy was at an end, so he would be with the Merchant Navy, the only thing, he told mother, was he would be on less money, then mother started, here we go, i thought, making my way to the stairs ready to run, 'And what the fuckin ell am i supposed ter do with this fuckin lot she roared, meaning us, you would think we enjoyed living there, 'Well yer will just av ter carry on the way you have been won't yer!'

'And there won't be as much leave as the Royal, he said, then he was gone, Again. 'All we heard for days,' was bastard this, and bastard that, when mother noticed he had not left her any money, 'How the fuck do i pay the rent,?' it hadn't been payed for eight weeks, Thats when we found out, we were getting evicted. Mother was beside her-self, there was nothing she could do about it, just accept it.

The night before we had to be out, mrs O'Brian who lived next door told mother she could leave as much of her stuff in her cellar, which was everything more or less, just leaving as much as we could each carry, which wasn't much, with the kids as well, it was done this way then, because the bailiffs who made sure you left just threw everything in the front garden, then locked the place up with steel so no-one could get in. That's how people knew you had been evicted, and Mrs O'Brian wanted to save mother that humiliation so she let us stay at her house, but only for a couple of days. As they watched the house being boarded up, MR O'Brian put his arm round mother's shoulder, he shouted to the onlookers, 'yer can all go in now, yer nosey shower o bastards'.

Mother looked at us and said with venom, 'yer can blame yer fuckin dad fer this', "what bloody dad"! He was no dad to me. I could count on my ten tiny fingers how many times we had seen him.

PART FIVE

～

THE DINGLE LIVERPOOL

After staying at the O'Brian's for three day's we were on the move again, carrying anything we could, mother was in Liverpool, she would only come back when it was dark, in case we were seen, she told us not to play out, because we would have been taken away and put into care, and looking back on my time spent in the dingle, i don't know if i would have rather gone into a home, but you would think that you could trust family, wouldn't you,? Oh how wrong i was. Mother had found two of father's cousin's, who lived in Hill Street and Carle Garden's, This is when i have to change the surnames because of their children, but they would have known by our surname who we were anyway, I just don't want to embarrass them. It was Irene who was to be the one who lived at the very bottom of Hill Street, next door to a chip-shop, her sister Maureen lived just facing in Carle Gardens and was married to Brian Hughes, he was nice Brian, so was Maureen, but it was Irene's children, who i was to look after, when Irene was at work, which was only next door anyway, and nine times out of ten, the kids would be in bed anyway. Her husband John used to play the guitar in all the pubs along the dock road, and was out most nights. Mother said it would only be for a couple of weeks, while she looked for rooms to live in. She started looking the day after we got there, but she was told if she wanted somewhere decent, she should try Parliament Street because the houses were bigger and let to people as rooms. After looking all around the area, she had to settle for two rooms over a shop in Upper Hill street, which was one room—cum living room, plus one other to be a bedroom, but up to now, it was a storeroom full of boxes, which would be moved before we moved in, the kitchen was a sink and a cooker which stood on the landing, and also had to be shared by two other people, who lived over us, even though we never saw anyone all the time we were there, the only draw-back was there was no toilet, only a shed in the yard with no light, 'Im not bleedin goin down there', yer can piss off,' yer don't fuckin know who's been on that. And so when mother made her mind up, that we would have to live there, it was decided, that Me, Teresa, Ann, and Harry were all to share the one room, two to a bed, Teresa's gob roared, don't fuckin think yer sleeping with me you, she said to me, you and him, meaning harry, can share an our Ann can sleep with me.!' Aye you, you don't tell me what ter fuckin do', she 'fuckin does enough o that', so you can fuck off', 'how easy it was to pick up the lingo then', it was the only language i was brought up on, it was only a matter of time before we all used it. 'I'd rather sleep on the floor, bitch,. In the end, me and harry topped and tailed, one at the top and one at the bottom, with a bucket in in the corner, just in case.

The owner of the shop was to be called Mr Ali, he was a Muslim and he stank to high heaven, he wore a white overall coat, which was as dirty and filthy as he was, and he scared the shit out of me. That coat must have been bloody painted on him, because he had the same one on every day, it looked as slimy as he did, there was something about him, the eye's were evil, it makes me sick to even think about it now. Worst of all, his stockroom was below the room where the four of us had to sleep, but when we noticed there were holes in the floor boards, that scared us so much, even the 'bitch' was scared, was when we found out he was watching, as we undressed, he was a fuckin pervert, we couldn't believe he was spying on us. It was understandably scary, and to make matters worse, he insisted that the bulbs should be dimmed because if it was too bright, we used too much electric, it must have felt bad to mother, she was really worried, which was a first,! We were told to take the so-called mattresses of the beds, and told by mother, we all should stay in the one room until she could get money for bolts to put on the doors and covered the holes up in the floor. We didn't know if she was worried about us or herself, but if we needed the bucket through the night, we had to go into the other room, but in pairs, then in the morning, we had to take the bucket down two flights of stairs and empty it from the night before, and we were terrified because we had to wait until slime-ball left his stockroom. Mother had not left any address with anyone in Kirkby, in case father came home, and wouldn't know where to find us, but we thought she had done it out of spite, because of the way he left us, she didn't want to be found. A few days later, mother had a visitor coming to see her, so she wanted all of us there' we were all shuttled in the corner like lost sheep, sitting on a mattress. 'I had promised Irene id babysit that day, but mother insisted i stayed where i was, 'Irene can wait, she said. Then the noise on the stairs told us that someone was coming up, more than one person, mother got up to answer the door, before they had even got the top of the stairs. 'Mrs O' Prey they asked, 'yeh' that's me she said, do you want to come in? You could see their noses twitching at the smell of the place, the stench of the place, was over-powering, but they were more surprised when they saw the state we were all in. The man and woman were from the National Assistants Board, more commonly known now as the DHSS. Mother told them she didn't know where father was, and the reason why we were evicted from the house in Kirkby, they were there for nearly an hour, and a cock and bull story from mother, but before they left, mother was given a money order to pay Mr Ali direct, then she was given vouchers for clothes for all of us, plus other stuff she would need for the place, including new beds, one each, 'Wow! 'That its self was a luxury in its self, we had never had a bed each, were was she gonna put them, but we need not have bothered worried, as soon as she could, mother only kept two and sold the others, surprise, surprise, bet you can guess who got one though, the 'bitch'. The vouchers she had to give Mr Ali, the slime ball, to get food and coal, also she owed him money for stuff she had got on tick. I was put into ST PATRICKS school, while harry, was in the same school, but the boys were another part. Teresa was told to find work, as she was now too old for school, so when MR ALI said he would give her a job, mother was over the bleedin moon, after all, she only had to walk down two flights of stairs, 'sooner her than me, i thought. I had to go straight to cousin Irene's after school to babysit, but mother said she had found me a cleaning job three afternoons a week after school, and it depended on what time i finished, then i could go to Irene's. 'And don't forget' he's got ter give yer five bob,' you can av a shilling, she was all heart was mother, 'What der yer mean he? 'Im not cleaning fer a bleedin man, not round here, their all as dirty as im downstairs, im not doin it, 'Just do as yer fuckin told,' he's an old man and he's on his own.

As i walked out of our entry, his house was four doors down, making my way up the stairs, i was met in the dark hallway, i was met by a woman, then known as Marge who seemed ok, friendly in fact who told me where i would find MR ROBINSON, the man i was to clean for, so nervously i made my way down to the cellar, 'can't all be like that, i thought, but they were, they were always dimmed. I knocked on the door, when i heard a voice ask 'Who is it? I answered who i was and that my mother had told me to call, he came to the door, everywhere was in darkness, including him, i I'm not racist by any means, but that was the first time i had ever seen a black man, and he scared the shit out of me, his voice was like a moan and i was about to turn round and run, when he told me to come in. Once again, the place was very dimmed, and you couldn't see your hands in front of you, i couldn't see him at all, and when i asked if i could have the light on to clean, he said no, but i could have a candle which was placed i the centre of a big ole fashioned table littered with odd coins and notes, of which i had only seen once before, not knowing they were five pound notes.

Just, when i asked him did he want me to move it, because the cloth he had on the table was full of clutter, i thought he was gonna bleedin eat me 'No No, Don't you touch that' his voice was very deep and loud, i couldn't understand a word he said, 'You go, Now! I was too scared to ask, but i had to, 'What about the money? I asked, and he threw two half crowns at me then pushed me out the door, i didn't need telling twice, i bent over to pick the coins up and ran up the stairs and out of the door, just before i got to the door, the woman called Marge said' Don't worry luv, he always shouts like that, 'Not at me i said, yer could have bleeding warned me.

I legged up the entry and up the stairs, 'all i needed was to bump into the slime ball, i was already shaking, from the old get round the fuckin corner. I walked in the 'living room, mother was sat or rather slumped on the chair by the fire, 'nothin new,' but there was, she was drunk, she was that pissed, she never even noticed she had burnt her legs, with Ann fast asleep and Carol sat in a dirty piece of cloth for a nappy, soaking wet and full of shit, it was then i threw a cup at her, that woke her up. "What the fuckin ell are yer doing?" although i was just going on thirteen, i was learning words that i had never heard before, because it's what i was brought up on, even now, i could put a docker to shame, because i swear like a trooper, and if anyone who knows me doesn't like the way i talk, then i tell them "What they see is what they get," because i tell people straight, one thing i am not, is a hypocrite, and so when i threw the cup at mother she sobered up alright, then she took the poker which was constantly in the coal fire, and she launched it right at me, so it was red hot, and if i hadn't pulled my knees up, the poker would have got me right between the eyes, so as it happend, it got me in the knee and it burnt a hole in my knee and iv' still got the hole in my leg to this day, then the next day, the bitch took me to Myrtle Street children's hospital and told them i had fell on a piece of barbed wire.! 'You had to give her credit, just for her tales, she should have had a degree, she came out with some cracker's, il give her that!

PART SIX

∞

Teresa only stayed at her job downstairs for just three weeks, telling mother she had found an all day job, but i was never told what she had said to mother, all i got told was she wouldn't be able to work for Mr Ali because of the hours she had to work, and only get half of what she was told she would get, and that was the main reason she didn't want to work for him anymore. It didn't bother me, i didn't give a shit, not then anyway, the longer she worked the better, because we never did get on, we were always pulling each other's hair out and fighting. I still had my cleaning job for Mr Robinson, but he only started to use a dim bulb after i told him i wouldn't work in the dark, how can i see what i was doing "What is it with these people,? Everyone had to have dimmed lights, but i was soon to find out, to my horror. I still only cleaned for him three times a week, but he never seemed to move out of the chair, and if he did, it was only to go to bed or use his "piss-pot", which i had constantly told him i wouldn't touch, that he could see to that himself, i was already his skivvy thanks to mother. On the third visit of the week, i asked him if i could have my money, he growled at me, as he grabbed me and threw me onto the bed, then he jumped on top of me and started to try and pull my knickers down, i screamed and kicked, then he put a hand over my mouth, and started to move up and down on me, even though all my clothes were all intact, i was petrified so the minute he let me go, i screamed the fuckin place down, until Marge from upstairs came running in the room, 'GET the fuckin ell of er, yer fuckin dirty old bastard!, she belted him over the head with a poker, then i lost my balance, the next thing i knew, i was in the hospital and there was a policewoman talking to mother, while a doctor was looking after me, I had to stay in overnight, because of the bang to my head, plus i was concussed. The policewoman said she would call and see me later that night, 'Just you rest love' 'You had a bad cut, they had to stitch it, so you'll have a bad head for a few days, il just av a word with your mother, then il come back and see how you are, ok! Something, by the look on mother's gob, i would be far from ok, there was more to come, but for that night, i would be ok. The nurse who was sitting with me, brought me a nice cup of hot chocolate and some dry biscuits, just in case i was sick, then the doctor came and told me to try and sleep, but i woke up crying, so he gave me some medicine to swallow, and the next thing i knew, mother was there to take me home. As she was trying to look as though she cared, the doctor who had stitched my head, came to tell mother how to tend to the cut, he said to me, 'Look young lady, 'No more bunking of school, and always tell your mother where you are,! The poor woman has been worried all day because she couldn't find you! That fuckin bitch! She had told the Police that i was bunking of school with other kids, Oh god, how i hated that woman.

That was the time i was to go and stay at Cousin Irene's, and was i glad about that. Irene's husband John, wanted to go and kill the man that did that to me, but Irene told him to leave it, because i was scared enough.

'Just tell me where he lives girl, the dirty bastard, il fuckin kill him,' john said.' 'No please john, don't, he might come looking fer me, I had been there a week, when mother came to Irene's and she had that woman called Marge, the one who lived in the house where the dirty get lived, 'Hello girl, i just wanted ter see yer,' are yer feeling any better? Then Irene butted in, 'The poor kid's terrified ta go out', I hope the bastard gets what's coming to him. 'He already has girl, my feller worked him over good style, the only problem is that he threw us out, the same night because he was arrested, but yer 'ma' told the police that she had sent you to stay at yer uncle's in Huyton, so they had to let him go, but yer needn't worry luv, he won't show his face anywhere.

Then Irene tore into my 'mother, 'Anyway Mary, what the fuck was she doin there in the first place?, you had her cleaning there when she should have been in school,' she's only fuckin thirteen fer God's sake.

'Oh Jesus, here we go, im in shit now, 'mother' didn't know id told Irene why i was there in the first place'. The look i got should have turned me to stone, but she told Irene that it was me that wanted to do it, for 'pocket money' and that id been bunking of school to do it! I never even knew what pocket money was, but Irene was ready for her, 'Don't give me no shit yer bitch' I've already been up the school, and as far as they know, yer told them yerself that she had gone to live with one of yer brother's', but they know the truth now, and she won't be going back to you. 'Everyone was right about you' and her father will know the truth when he gets home!

'Harry doesn't know where we are, mother said', 'He does now' ive been down to the seamen's mission, to make sure he knows. The blood drained from 'mother's face, and he's gonna know the whole lot, so till he gets home, she stays here. 'Oh God, i thought, that's all i need . . . . But nothing prepared me for what was comin next.

After a couple of months at Irene's, I had never been happier, Irene would take me out every Saturday, to the market and she would buy me certain things, clothes-wise, but something different every week, this particular week, it was all under-ware, she was also the only one who had ever bought me my first bra, 'I think yer need ta be wearing one now girl' yer got more up there than iv got, she laughed. That's what mothers are supposed to buy for their girls but not mine, as i looked at all what Irene had bought me, i started to cry, which kicked her off, the two of us sat there by the fire, she was more like a mother to me than my own was, and i wished i could have lived with her forever. 'Come on girl, im gonna be late fer work', 'Will yer be ok with the kids fer a couple of hour's only John as gorra go out fer a couple of hour's but i should be in by then, im only next door anyway if yer need me, but the kids should sleep anyway, 'thats ok, i said, they are good for me anyway.

At five o'clock, John and Irene left at the same time, both telling me not to open the door to anyone, and they had their keys, so all i had to do was sit and watch the telly they had bought. This was the first time i had ever seen one, it was very small in a dark wooden surround and showed black and white, but it was something to watch, and john said the price wasn't bad, seeing as though it 'fell off the back of a lorry'. I went upstairs, just to check on the kids, but they were fast asleep as normal, but they were good kids anyway, not a bit of trouble.

John was back home, he'd only been gone an hour, but he said he had to come home to get changed, as he was playing for a wedding 'do' so he went upstairs and i just carried on watching the telly, 'See yer later girl' tell Irene i might be a bit late will yer doll? 'Ok, i shouted back, then, i heard the front door close. About ten minutes later, i heard one of the kids crying which was unusual, so i was going into the bedroom where they were, when i heard a noise coming from the back room, which was called the attic, but i always thought the attic was at the very top, anyway i just peeped my head round the door, but the kids were sound asleep, so i thought there was maybe a window open or something, i knew i'd heard some kind of noise, i went over to check the window, which was slightly open so after i'd closed it, i was on my way out of the room when, something was thrown over my head, and i was being told if i opened my mouth, that he would kill me and i was being dragged backwards into the room and the door being closed but not banged shut. Then i was told to get on the floor, i never recognised the voice, but it was very deep and croaky, and for a slight second, i thought the old dirty bastard from Upper hill street had found me and waited until everyone had gone out, he must have been watching the house,' He's found me, and now he's gonna kill me for getting the police onto him,' Then i was raped, i was too scared to move, even when it was over, i was told 'Shut yer mouth an don't turn round' then he was gone. I lifted myself up slowly looking round the room as i did, but scared so when i got the chance, i went and closed the window, Then i sat in the corner and sobbed my heart out. 'Why me, why me?. But i couldn't come up with any answers. 'Is this all my life is gonna be?'As i stood up, i felt funny, my head was swimming, it was then i noticed all my legs were full of blood, i ran into the toilet, the knickers what Irene had bought me were ruined so i flushed them down the toilet, i could have tried to wash them but i couldn't bare to touch them. After i gave myself a good wash down, i put clean knickers on, with my nightdress, another present of Irene, i just sat there with the television on, but not watching it, my mind was replaying what had gone on the last hour, not wanting to think, but my mind had other idea's of its own, then it hit me! 'That wasn't the old man, because for one, he didn't have a Liverpool accent, plus whoever it was, he couldn't have climbed through the window, which was the only way anyone could have got in, so it must have been a burglar, it must have been". I was relieved to think he hadn't found me, but still scared to think how whoever it was, had got in, because if it happend then, it could happen again and knowing that sent shivers down my spine.

I must have fell asleep, the next thing i knew, Irene was talking to me, 'Come girl, iv brought yer some scallops the last ones in on a Saturday night, when the pubs close.' 'I think we could both do with an early night anyway'. Isn't John in yet? He's not this late any other time, 'oh he said he'd be a bit late, i told her, he had to come home and get changed because he had a wedding to do or something, i was so heavy-eyed, i couldn't care less what time he got home. 'Oh sod him then, he won't be home yet, an im not waiting up fer im, 'im bloody knackered so are you,' come on girl, let's be avin yer, then just as we were about to go up the stairs, we heard his key in the lock, 'Are aye lad, we were just goin ter bed, madam er was fast asleep when i got in, an im tired me-self, so if yer want somethin to eat, yer'l av to do it yerself.' 'Don't worry doll, im full anyway, they ad everythin at that wedding. 'What wedding? Irene asked, didn't yer tell her? He pointed to me, 'sorry i forgot, i said. 'Oh by the way, what were yer doin climbing up the bleedin drainpipe? 'Yer soft get, yer could av broke yer bleedin neck', my head turned as fast as he looked at me! 'It was Les who saw yer, so he told her, 'Your stupid cat, was hanging out the bleedin window, if i hadn't got it, he'd be brown bread now! But he knew i was on to him, his look of fear told me who raped me, he couldn't wait to get out the room quick enough. 'Anyway, come on, it's late let's get to bed. As we left the living room, Irene went to check everything was as it should be, 'Il fuckin av you,' yer nothin better than that dirty old bastard up the road,' 'but you won't get away with it,' il make sure yer don't.

I knew then that i couldn't stay there anymore and it broke my heart, although Irene was my second cousin, she was as dear to me as my lovely aunty tre, i knew i couldn't tell her what a dirty, horrible, filthy bastard her husband was, i couldn't hurt her like that, but she would want to know why i was leaving, and i knew as much as i wanted to, i couldn't bring myself to tell her.! I waited until everyone was asleep, then picking up my bag with everything Irene had bought me inside, i left Irene a small note' just to say 'thank you' and if she wanted to know why i had left, then she should ask her husband, i knew he would come up with some cock an bull story, but i wonder, even to this day if she ever found out, but as i said earlier, going by the verse he put in the paper, that the bastard was still up to his dirty tricks, till she died, and i hope he fuckin rots in hell, at least now, Irene has at last found the peace she so deserved. "REST IN PEACE CUZ".

I didn't go back to 'mother' no way was i goin back to her, at least with a rape, it was over in minutes, but going back to her was a life sentence, when all i had done was to be born, but walking round, early hours of the morning, in a place full of Muslim's and black people, i was petrified of them, thats when i took a bottle of sleeping tablets, after all, if this was all i had to looked forward to in life, then "Why would i want to live?

PART SEVEN

∞

The next thing i knew, i was being sick, Someone had found me, slumped in a shop doorway on the Scottie Road, god knows how i got there, probley trying to find my aunty tre, but she didn't live there anymore and i had forgot. As it turned out, i was found early the next morning, by a cleaner going to work, who then got the police and ambulance and i was then rushed to the children's hospital in the town called The Northern.

There were police and doctor's everywhere, the nurses making me swallow some medicine to make me throw up, i had been scared when i saw a black man coming toward me, then when he sat down next to me, i lost the plot, because i was so scared of him, when they asked where i lived, and me being a thick shit, i only went and give 'mothers' address' then bit my lip in temper. I still am a bit unsure about being in certain places, but I'm certainly not racist, not at all.

I was kept in for a week, but i told them i didn't want 'mother' there, and i couldn't tell them that i was supposed to be at Irene's, no way. There was a man in a suit who came to see me every day, whom i now know was a social worker, but they were not called that back then, and when 'mother' did show, it was to be taking my stuff down the back allies, to the shop's back door, and that's when i knew where i was going back to.

As soon as we got to the rooms where we lived, or rather where i used to live, my skin started to crawl, and i couldn't stop shaking, and crying. 'It's yer own fuckin fault, yer stupid bastard! She said to me, but this time i answered her back, 'Do yer think i fuckin wanted to come back here or to you i roared at her!? 'You little cunt' she said, i thought that's a new one. "Who the fuckin hell are you fuckin swearing at? She belted me, giving me another bruise, 'I fuckin hate you' i told her, and if yer think yer gonna 'hire' me out again, think again, because i have only got ter go to the phone box, so yer better watch yerself, i told her, feeling proud of myself for standing up to her! I had been back half an hour then she started, firstly she took the parcel i had, my clothes, as she did once before when i was with my aunty tre. I started to push her away, then i got the poker across my knee, so as i was cowered in the corner, i thought, how i hated that woman, 'You can fuck off,' these will do Teresa, I grabbed my parcel and tried to sit on it, then just as she was about to leather me again when there was a loud knock at the door, then as she went to see who it was, i managed to grab some vest's and knickers, which i put on, just as father walked in.! Dropping his kit bag on the floor, he headed straight for his precious son, not taking a blind bit of notice of the rest of us, it was only when Carol cried that he realised we were there. What's up with them? he said, 'Oh just leave them', their just tired. 'How did yer find me? she asked him, 'the mission gave me our Irene's address and she told me, 'whats been goin on with that one? meaning me, 'Oh she's caused no end of trouble, that little shit, she's always bleedin running away, never goes ter school or she gob's off at anyone who try's ter tell er ter do somethin and then gets the cane or sent home.! She could have been an actress, the things she came out with, you couldn't make it up, she was that good, but i never said a word, because i was scared of getting the buckle of his belt, which i remember so well. 'Well, she's only a kid' she'll learn' and then she'll meet her match'. Anything to eat Moll,? Im bloody starving he said,' what about them? 'Oh their gettin ready fer bed now, they've had their tea, the lying bitch i thought, then he opened his bag and came toward us, handing each of us a bar of caramac chocolate, a lousey bar of bleeding chocolate, from a man who claimed to be a father when we didn't even know him, nor could he remember our names, he was horrible and i hated his guts.

He then said to mother, 'Come girl, iv only got the weekend' we were waiting for her to start, but she never said a word, she just made her face up adding a bit of lipstick, which made no difference anyway, she was still an ugly bitch, as far as i was concerned anyway. We were all asleep till we were woken up by voices on the stairs, we thought it was them coming back from the pub, but mother came into the room crying and telling Teresa to get up and watch the baby, because she had to go the hospital with father, on hearing these words, i jumped up, asking what was wrong with him, but got told to shut up! Fuck yer, i thought and turned over to go back to sleep. The following morning, mother told us that father had suffered a heart attack, but he was ok, 'pity i thought' trust him to get better. I know that anyone who might read this and think i was a heartless bitch, then start reading again! Then, you might forgive me for not 'Caring' . . .

Later in the afternoon, mother was going back to the hospital, SEFTON GENRAL, it was called, so teresa was given order's to watch the kids, 'Cheeky cow, she's not telling me what ter do, she's only just over a year older than me. An hour later, mother was back, she needed to take him some clean underwear in, he did'nt have any pyjamas so he would have to make do with the hospital gown, she moaned, then she set off again for the afternoon visit. He was sitting up in bed, smoking when she got there, 'There's yer Cigs, she said almost throwing them at him,' did yer get me echo girl' he asked, 'Oh shit arry, i can't remember everything, i forgot, il go and get yer one in a bit,' just let me av a cig and take these shoes off fer a bit', me bleeding feet are killing me. Then she must have thought he'd forgot about his paper or she hoped he'd forgot, but he didn't, she was telling him that she wouldn't be able to go back on the night-time visit, because her feet were bleeding from all the walking she'd had to do, when he butted in 'Oh aye girl, will yer just pass me the echo in before yer go, an if yer not comin back, il av nothin ter read. 'Bloody ell,' il go and get it now,' she called him all the names under the sun, 'He's got the bleeding life of a lord, and as bleedin always, i get the run around, stupid fuckin paper.'

As she was about to walk back into the ward to give him his bloody paper, she was stopped by a nurse, and being told to sit down, the doctor wanted to see her, but i only came back to give him his paper she said' 'What's wrong,? 'What's happend? Then she stood up to see why the curtain's were pulled around his bed, then she saw four doctor's come from his bed, but leaving the curtain shut. They told her that he had another heart attack, but this time it was a massive one and they did all they could to save him, but they couldn't. 'Mother' was in total shock, 'But iv only been gone ten minuet's she told them, the nurse was trying to get her to drink sweet hot tea, which was supposed to help with shock, but she just waved it away.

They knew that they couldn't let her go home alone, not in that state anyway, so they had to get the police to come and take her home, asking if she had anyone that could stay with her, because of the shock, she should not be on her own, not now. The only one we could think of, was Irene, his cousin . . . .

PART EIGHT

∞

I was the one that had to go and see Irene, and i was so scared that i might bump into John, or even the black man, the slime ball that was our landlord, even worse, i had to face Irene, which i dreaded, 'What if she asks me about what john had done, but she never did, she probley knows what he did or at least she had an idea, but she said nothing, just that she would let father's parents know, and that was it. 'I only hoped she didn't blame me' but then i was told that when you die, you know everything about the life you left behind, so if she didn't know then, she will now that she's passed. I really hope she knows.

The night that father had died, mother just sat there, staring into space, and not a tear was shed, she only opened her mouth when she wanted something, or to shout at us, and to all intent and purpose, you wouldn't think there was anything changed, except she was a little more quiet than normal, which that in itself was creepy, as we didn't know when she was gonna blow. I should have known it was too good to be true, because she came toward me and that was when she blew up, i just happend to be in the wrong place at the wrong time, bloody typical, it had to be me, didn't it? It was all over the stuff i had took from the parcel of clothes that i had brought from Irene's the week before, i thought she had forgot about them, but i was wrong, 'Again' i couldn't bleeding win. But to my surprise, after she got stuck into me, dragging my hair out, breaking my two front teeth, little harry dived on her back, screaming at her to leave me alone, 'What the bloody ell is up with him,? I thought, normally he didn't give a shit, he was the little blue eye, even Teresa had her nose pushed out which she wasn't too happy about, 'i only took a pair of knickers i cried' then with a big clump of my hair in her hands, she sat down and sobbed and sobbed. The next day, mother's sisters, Margaret and Vera, and one of her brothers turned up, Uncle George, with whom Vera lived with in Birmingham, then one by one, all of them would take it in turn's to stay with mother, to offer support and help with us kids. It was decided that i was to go and stay with my aunty Margaret and her husband Stan, who lived in Tuebrook, it could have been on the bleedin moon for all i knew, id never heard of it, but i wasn't gonna argue, But we all had to be back, just for the day of 'Fathers funeral' which was to be at his sister's flat in Beaumont Street, "There was no way a brother of hers was lying in a coffin in this hell hole" said his sister Mary! Uncle George said he would take Teresa and harry, but he would have to sort it with his wife Ann, who was a proper Birmingham lass and Vera could get Teresa a job where she worked. HENRY JOSEPH O'PREY, PASSED AWAY MARCH 25TH AGED 37.1962. Everything was real, now mother saw the announcement in the Liverpool echo, with other verses from his side of the family, none from her side, except that he left behind a wife and five children.

    A policeman came the day after he died, to bring to mother, fathers belongings and personal stuff that had been at the police station until after his death. All this had got to mother, who then fell to the floor and everyone running to her, but she wouldn't cry, not in front of these she wouldn't. Uncle George told mother, he had to get back, but he would be back in time for father's funeral, which was to take place at the beginning of the following week, and also to tell his wife ANN to make Arrangement's to take me and harry, but it would take a bit of time, because he had three kids of his own, and when he had rescued Vera, from their father, they had to build a small box-room for her, and because this was once the bathroom, they had the bathroom added to the kitchen downstairs, but told mother not to worry, he would sort it.

    Mother had to go to the National Assistance Board, to get help toward the cost of the funeral and help for clothes, because none of us possessed anything fit to go to a funeral, we had nothing full stop. On the day of the day of the funeral, everyone was crying, but that didnt worry us, and mother not looking forward to seeing father's, sisters, but we'd never seen them before anyway, why should we be arsed.? We made our way there by a taxi, all of us dressed in black, there were a few people standing round, just talking and waiting for the coffin to come out, as we got there, mother told us to go and pay our last respects to father, we had never been to a funeral and didn't know what she meant, we said no, 'I didn't want to see a dead body' father or not, then his sister Mary, took us in the room where the coffin was, and she made us kiss his face, which scared the shit out of me, and because i said no, she smacked me right across the face, leaving finger marks. I waited for mother to say something to her, but she didn't give a shit, so i was held down and made to kiss a man i had hated and hardly knew anyway, it was the most scariest things i had to do, it was like kissing a cold candle and i threw up everywhere in front of everyone, which didn't please Mary. After everything was over, we went straight home as we were not invited to attend 'the wake' we didn't even know what that meant at the time.

There was one more night left for us, to spend at them rooms as a so-called family, before we all got separated and we all got 'Farmed' out to other family members, and i couldn't wait, little harry was sitting in the corner with little Ann, when suddenly she went toward them, she picked the baby up, carol, then Ann and Teresa, she walked over to the little rug she had in front of the fire, then she sat down and just hugged them, Teresa turned round at me and harry and she gave us the most evil smirk i had ever seen, she had her precious mother back, all to herself, she was truly evil. 'What the fuckin hell are you looking at, she said to me and harry, which was odd, because father had doted on his son, and now she hated the sight of him, it was as if she blamed him for fathers death,! As she stood up and started to walk toward us, i flinched, but harry just stared at her and he wouldn't move, not even when she told him to. 'Well are yer two little bastards happy now? Mother launched at harry, belting him all over the place, just to hear him cry, but the more she hit him, the harder he became and he would not give her the satisfaction of seeing him cry, she then turned to me and i thought 'here we go' it's my turn,' but all she did was tell me, i wasn't worth her breath, 'charming woman' wasn't she? Roll on tomorrow i thought, then with anything she could lay her hands on, she threw at me and harry and screamed at both of us, to get the fuck out of the room and stay out, 'only happy to' i thought!

At nine o'clock on the dot, aunty Margaret turned up with her husband Stan, all ready ter go girl, were are yer clothes, i grabbed my little 'bag' which mother had said that was all i could take, i ran over to the bed, were she had hidden the stuff i got of Irene, and she had forgotten about on the night father had came home, but i didn't forget, she can't do anything to me now i thought, not with these two here, and the look of contempt on her face was a picture, i smirked at her as i walked out of that room for the last time. I was told to call Stan, uncle Ron,' but i thought yer name was Stan' i said, but aunty Margaret told me that he was only called that because his surname was Stanley, so everyone where he worked just called him that, but his real name was Ronald, so thats what i was to call him, while i was living with them anyway, i was so happy, and even happier when i found out that they had two little boys who were twins, called John and David and only a few weeks old. Uncle Ron worked on the buses, and whenever we went to meet him after work, he always finished at his depot, in Green Lane, just by Old Swan, and he would always make a fuss of me, and i thought 'oh no, not again', but i was worrying about nothing, it's just the way he was, he was nice, and they lived in a street called Buckingham Road. The house was massive and it was lovely, it was like a mansion, but i was told that they had the rooms downstairs and a proper kitchen, their living room and bedroom were next door to each other, but the only thing they had to share was, the bathroom on the middle floor. It was also the home of Billy and Marline RATHBONE, who i was to become very close to in the few years to come, but that's another story!

I loved living with aunty Marge, as i called her, i loved everything about being part of her 'family', i loved going to the small shop on the corner, taking the babies for walks just up and down the road, or to the shop, but most dogs, even to this day, she was a lovely gentle giant, which would explain why I have always had dogs since as far as i can remember, anyway, i was as happy as Larry, being at aunty Margaret's, it always gave me pleasure to do anything for her. I loved cleaning, not that it needed doing because it was like a palace, albeit it only two room's and a kitchenette, most of all i loved doing the washing up, because there was always hot soapy water, i used to take my time because i wasn't used to hot water, the room they called the living room, was really tiny, and my bed was the sofa, but even that was better than what i had been sleeping on at that bitch's. I was thirteen, going on thirty Margaret said to me, 'yer a little old woman on legs yer are girl. One day, she had sent me to the shop on the corner, just to get her some cig's, i had started to smoke then, so every now and again, Marge would give me one, 'but don't tell Ron, she would say, so when i wanted one, i would ask if i could take the kids or the dog for a walk, but she always knew why i wanted to go out. I was coming out of the shop one way, i was a bit in front, so i started to walk a bit faster, and as i got to the door, he stopped and looking at me, he started up the stairs after me,' 'i hope yer not following me' i told him, 'my aunty lives her' 'So does mine, he said, it's my aunty Marlene, are you Margaret's niece? 'yes i am, i told him, i was shaking badly, because of all that had happend to me in the past, it was hard for me to trust any man, but he was only young, older than me, but still, he was only young. He told me his name was Alan, and Marlene was his mum's sister, and that he came over every weekend to see her and her son, and Uncle Billy of course. He lived in Walton, just a walk away, The following day, i was sat on the front steps, playing with Mandy the dog, when he came down and sat beside me and we swapped stories, about each other, and although i was only thirteen, and unaware, i had just met my first ever boyfriend, by the name of Alan Gallagher, he was nearly eighteen, but it didn't bother him that i was only thirteen, soon to be fourteen, and very naive, but i knew he liked me, and me him, and from then, we were always together,!

PART NINE

∞

That house in Buckingham Road, and the people in it, will always hold a special place in that part of my life.

All the people in it loved me for who i was, and made me feel part of their family, at a time in my life when i needed their stable love, which they gave me freely, and for that i will never forget them. Alan and me were inseparable, before i moved there, he would only come over to his aunt Marlene's on a Friday because they would sometimes ask him to babysit their son, little Billy we used to call him, thats why Alan just came on a Friday, but like i said, all that changed when i moved there, from the first day we met, he would come over every night, after work. He worked in a place that delivered banana's, near Old Swan, and he used to always wear light blue drainpipe jeans with a crease as sharp as a knife, but no matter the weather, he would never wear a coat, there's an advert on telly which always reminds me of him, a washing powder when a son had to wash his own shirt, and that was Alan to a tea, every time, the shirt was snow white and blue jeans, i can still see that picture in my mind, even to this day. At first i was a bit nervous, when we went for walks, but he would just hold my hand, he never even tried to kiss me, because he knew my fears, but he understood and never put any pressure on me at all. I never knew what love was then, well not that kind of love anyway, and i would get butter-flies in my belly, which i never even understood, but it only ever happend when i saw him, so thats when i knew i felt something for him, but what or why, i never knew till i was older, but what i did know, was that i didn't want to be away from him.

Me and Alan would do everything together, and both our auntie's knew how close we had become, but nothing was said, they just accepted the fact. When we both had to babysit, depending on who it was, we would sit on the stairs and he would teach me to play cards, or we would wait until we thought everyone was asleep, he would sneak down the stairs, but mostly it would be me sneaking up, and all we did, as always was play card's, we would just sit or lie down on our bellies and play cards. We were more like mates, than boy and girlfriends and we were content with that. On the nights that we didn't babysit, Alan would take me swimming, in Queen's Drive, but the first time we wanted to go, aunty Marge took me up to Old Swan and bought me two swimming costume's, because swimming was later to be an obsession with me, i loved it, and the very first time ice skating was the same. He enjoyed teaching me, because it gave him the chance to get closer to me, and then when we stopped by the hand rails, i got my very first kiss, i didn't know if i was scared or did i like it? I knew at my age then, that i was too young to be kissed, but it was just a kiss, nothing more.

It was four glorious months i was with aunty Marge, then fate took over, and i was told that my stay there had come to an end, because Uncle George had been in touch, to say that he would be coming to collect me on the Saturday which meant i would have to go the day before, which was two days away, but a day i would never forget. I did nothing but cry and plead with everyone, to let me stay, 'Please, Please, i begged, let me stay here, but it was no use, that was all for nothing, my cries where not heard, but aunty Marge was tearful as well and she told me it was 'Mothers' decision, and that was the end of it. 'Fuckin bitch, fuckin bitch', that's all i called her, 'How that bitch has ruined my life, for the last time,' there's no way im going, no way', not now i had Alan.

Alan was at work on the day i was supposed to be going, and i started crying again, so i phoned his work's and told them i had to speak to him urgently, as soon as i heard his voice, i was still crying, then all i heard was the phone click, then nothing, i thought i might have got him in trouble for phoning him so pressed the 'B' button to get my pennies back, because if my plan would work, then i would need every penny i could get my hands on.

I started to walk back to aunty Marge's when i heard someone shouting, but i carried on walking taking no notice of anything, when all of a sudden i was grabbed from behind and was just about to lash out, when i looked into Alan's face! . . . 'Whats up? Whats up? He had only gone and walked out of work, thinking something had happend to me, 'They are sending me to live with my uncle,' i told him, 'please tell them Alan, please, i don't want to go, i want to stay here, with you, i don't want to leave you. His face dropped when i told him it was Birmingham, 'How long for? These were question's i couldn't answer, and i didn't know anyway, all i knew was i wanted to stay with him. He stayed with me till it was time for me to go, and they had to drag me away, but i wouldn't budge, but in the end i had to go, but for how long, no-one knew, me and Alan stood on our own for a while, just holding hands, then after we had swapped addresses, well he gave me his, but i didn't have a clue where i was going, but we promised to write every day, but he would have to wait till i knew the address where i was living, then i was gone, sobbing my heart out. The letter's started as soon as i got there, and carried on for ten months, and it was then i started to lose interest and the letters stopped, but once again, i didn't know what i was in for!.

Uncle George was nice, but his wife never let me forget, that she was doing me a favour, or rather my 'mother, Aunty Vera was still there, but she was getting married in three weeks time, so the box-room that was her room was given to me, she kept it lovely. Although the house only had two big bedrooms, the box-room was really for Paul, Uncle George's son, and his twin daughters, Heather and Caroline had the other bedroom, and Vera would bunk in with one of them till she got married, she didn't mind. George's wife was called Ann, and the bloke that Vera would be marrying was called Warren, who seemed ok, but thought himself God's gift to women. With the coming wedding, everyone was always in a rush, even aunty Ann, because all three of them worked all day, 'I was soon to become a 'skivvy' again but was to be called a godsend. 'Have i got dickhead written on my fuckin head? I asked myself, i was really getting pissed off now. Ann had sorted out the school i was going to, then she would come up with set of rules, 'rules for me' that was, the three kids were all under five and had to be taken to a babysitter every morning, which was a twenty minutes away at least, and that was only the start.

Every morning, i would take the kids, then pick them up again after school, but before that, every dinner time, i had to go back 'home', i would have to clean the house, all of it except their bedroom, i wasn't ever to go in there, a list would be made of things that i had to do, then get the tea ready, so all she had to do, was dish up, depending on what we were having, there was two more rules added to the list, I now had to get up before everyone else and clean the fire out, then start getting the kids ready. It was only when Vera opened her mouth and told Ann she was expecting me to do too much, it was then she declared that i would get two pound a week, she didn't fuckin ask for much did she.?

The school i was going to, was called Hands-worth Road, and it was mixed, and right facing WINSON-Green prison. It was common knowledge that i was a 'Scouser' then, and had people baffled the way i spoke, everyone wanted to be my friend, or have a peak, even the boys in the next school yard, especially when it was p-e because we had to do it in navy blue knickers, i thought it was degrading, because the boys got to wear shorts but we girls couldn't, then on a Friday, we had to walk all the way up Hands-worth Road to another school for a weekly exercise in a place called the annex, i hated going there, so it wasn't long before i started to skip school, and just drop the kids off then go back home, and i would do the jobs that i should have done after school, which would then give me some time for myself, but that was my down fall, because if Ann saw i had any spare time, then she would fill it, she was a devious bitch, she didn't like me, she made that quite clear, and the feeling was mutual. If she thought she could get away with anything, she would have a bleedin good try, now there was a rota for who would wash up after tea, and get different cereals ready for the next day, after my turn, i was allowed to go to the local park, 'but wait for it', as long as i took the twins with me, till it was their bed-time, crafty bleedin mare. The park was only down the road, known to the locals as Black-Patch park', and in one area there were slides, swings and anything kids could want, then on the other side, there was a massive boating lake, which i would just walk round with the pram. Things began to settle down as i adjusted to my surroundings, and the friends i had made at school, and a girl who was to become my best friend called Tracy Morgan, she lived in a place called Moseley, which was where i had to take the kids, and we used to pass each other every day, thats how we got talking, then sometimes she would walk with me, until she showed me the big swimming baths she went to. Well, that was school out the window, because the baths was always empty on week days, and we more or less have the place to ourselves, i was in heaven, and it was then i would think of Alan, my Alan, and how much i missed him, it was then i decided to run away, i had to get back to Liverpool at all costs, but how,? The girl i was knocking around with, Tracy came up with an idea, bunking on the train.

We decided to go the next week, because that would give us time to get some money, it was then i wondered why she said 'us', 'well im coming with you she said, you are not leaving without me, she said, but i didn't want her to come with me, so i had to think of something, fast.! The strain of what i had to do before and after school, was affecting my schooling and when i got home, Ann was waiting for me. "I have had to take time off work because of you" she said to me, 'and tomorrow,' she said it was because i had been caught bunking off school, and she told me that she had to take me to see the head teacher. It was that night i decided to run away the next day. I never got far, the guard who had already been told to watch out for me earlier by the police, caught me, i was taken to the police station, and went to fetch my uncle. I was taken home, in a side-car of a motorbike, and i felt ashamed, fancy being stuck in that thing,! It was a week later, when Vera got married and i found out that mother was coming, and the day after the wedding, she was also taking me home, back to Liverpool and my Alan, or was i going back, as Ann said. After the school, and the running away, i had been 'grounded', as Ann called it, if she could have tied my hands and feet together, she still wouldn't be happy, she was doing everything she could, to get me away, she even said i was stealing money out of uncle's pockets, but Vera had proof it wasn't me, because things were going wrong before i even got there, money had been going missing in the past because Vera caught her taking money, and other things. Vera used to have a wicker bag, in the shape of a lobster pot, and i found it fascinating, so every now and then, she would let me use it for school, and when i did borrow it, she always left two cigs in the bottom, she knew i smoked but never said anything, The one thing i did do, twice, was when Ann would send me over to the little shop to get whatever she wanted on 'tick', i would add an extra pack of cigs, Park Drive they were called, but i got caught the second time, thats when she told my uncle that she wanted me gone, but it was to be another two months before i was to go home, not when mother said, then i should have known she was lying again, but that was her.

As soon as Vera knew her own new house was ready, Warren, her soon to be husband, moved in it, but also because Vera didn't trust Ann, and wouldn't put nothing, past her. Three days before the wedding, Vera took me to see her new house, after she had been already, she had the place done through-out, with very thick carpet, curtains up and furniture already there, so all she had to was move in. It was beautiful, and looked like something out of a fairytale, the house was in the middle of know-where, surrounded by fields, a place called Cannock Chase, which is still known as the Black Country, and she couldn't wait to move in it!

As the big day loomed, people started to arrive the day before, but had to stay in small inn's scattered around the area, when mother arrived, she wouldn't look me in the face, nor did she want to, she had the offer of staying in the box-room with me and i froze, but she told uncle that she had already found somewhere to stay, with my aunty Margaret, who i was made up to see, and even more made up when she gave me a letter, saying 'I think yer know who thats from'. It was from Alan, asking me why i had stopped writing to him, when i thought it was him who stopped, because i had got too involved with friends i had made at school, not thinking how long it was when i last wrote to him, so he gave me his address again, and i was made up because i had lost it, it was right then i wrote to him, and gave the letter to aunty Marge so i knew he would get it. When uncle Jim and my lovely aunty Tre turned up, you could have cut the air with a knife, and i wasn't sure if anyone knew the story, and the only one i had told was Vera, and even then i wasn't sure she believed me, but when mother gave them a cold stare and completely ignored them, Vera looked at me, and i just shrugged my shoulder and went to give them a hug, which told Vera the truth about her so-called sister.

I was told i wouldn't be going to the wedding, although every other child was, as if i was bothered, i was just the skivvy don't mind me. The day after the wedding, everyone had gone home back to Liverpool, even mother, she never even came to see me, but even if she had, it would have worried me, because she never gave did give a shit about me. Three weeks later, we had just finished having tea, when there was a knock at the front door, we all looked at each other, no-one ever used that door. I didn't know who was more scared, me or Ann, 'Go on then' she said to me, i made my way through the parlour and opened the door only to get the shock of my life. It was Alan, and i screamed with delight. Wait there i told him, and when i told aunty Ann who it was, i asked could he come in for a cup of tea, "hes come all this way to see me", please i begged, "oh go on then, but no mess". We sat on the sofa and the word's just would'nt come, then they all came at once. "Is there anywere we can go" he said, I don't feel right sittin here, so when i asked if i could go out for half an hour, it was on condition that i took the twins with me. I didn't care, just that i could be with Alan, that's all that mattered. Then she said go out the back way, snob i thought, god forbid that anyone might see a strange bloke coming out her precious front door. On our way out, uncle George was just gettin in from work, so i told him who Alan was, and he said "ok girl, just make sure that bike is put in the yard', meaning Alan's motorbike, which we did, and off we went. On our way to Blackpatch Park, which was just down the road,

He said to me 'Are yer sure yer never got my letters? 'Because your uncle looks sound, but she seems like a right dragon'. 'He is nice, but yer right about her' she thinks im a skivvy, that's the only reason im here', and when i thought about that, It did make me think, would she keep my letter's? She would if she thought she would'nt get found out! Alan knew he had to use the 'softly softly' approach with me, because of my past, but i only told him that i was followed by a man, not all the gory bits, and he understood that. He promised he would come again, but he said, 'make sure yer tell that lot in the park, 'that you have got a proper boyfriend' and keep them letters comin'. And that was the last time i saw Alan Gallagher, but i didn't think he would come again, so when the letters stopped comin for what-ever reason, and everything just' went out of the window, so to speak, he was part of the happier time of my life, and i had to get on with life without him, or so i thought.

PART TEN

"GOING HOME"

My mother had been living with another of her brother's house in a place called HUYTON, somewhere called BARKBETH ROAD, when she had heard that father had left some kind of life insurance, the amount was two thousand pound, which was a bloody fortune, well in them days it was. You should have seen all her siblings come out of the woodwork then, they all wanted to be her friend. Norma, mothers sister in-law, was a well formed woman, in all description, was a very happy go lucky woman, who also had three kids, always laughing, and was never happier when she was with her kids. Anyway, as i was saying, mother had this money, and the first thing she did was to pay the rent she owed, the reason we were evicted from Kirkby months before she knew it, she was offered a brand new house and would be a least three weeks till we could move in, but Norma, being the lovely soul that she was, told mother to get me home, 'After all, it's only fer a couple of weeks, an im sure we can sort somethin out girl'. The next thing i knew, i was packing my stuff, I was going home, wondering if this was another sly trick of mothers, but 'yeh, i was going home, where-ever home was at that time. I was met at the railway station by mother and Norma, i didn't know if i should have laughed, cry, or be scared, but thankful to be away from the guard who uncle George had asked to keep an eye on me, anyway, mother came toward me and put her arm round me, now i was scared, because that was the first time in my life she had ever hugged me, ever. That was the only time i was happy to see mother. All in all, we were all living at 'Norma's house, 'she said in a joke, 'Don't call me aunty cos it makes me feel old', anyway we were there for two months, only so she could get the house ready and sort furnishings out and everything was ready, then all we had to do was move in. Norma and uncle Frank, were lovely and the house was full of love and laughs all the time, they just seemed to bounce of each other, i didn't know if they were serious or joking, but then they would look at my face and burst out laughing, it was like that all the time and i got used to it.

I got to know the girl next door, her name was June, June Forsyth and within the space of a few weeks, we became close friends, we went everywhere together and even dressed the same. I remember when i first got there, mother gave me a big box and told me to open it, and inside was a big portable radio, 'Ghetto Blasters' they were called, it was bloody massive, but i loved it, purely because it was the first thing she had ever bought me. 'Well, do yer like it? I didn't know what to say or do, for the first time i can remember, i was stuck for words then, there was a group called the Beatles, who wore coats with half cut collars, and these coats we got at the princely sum of six pound, which again was a fortune then. When me and June went out at nights, we were at that age when we got interested in boys, nothing major, just hanging around with them and everywhere together. We were to find out what a wardrobe was, but as it turned out she had meant clothes, not the wooden type, she rigged me out from top to toe, three times over, i had never seen so many clothes, and no, i didn't have to share them, i had never been so happy, and then i swore i would never call her 'mother' again, i would call her mam, but nothing is too good to last, but that was when i learned to keep my mouth shut, for the time being anyway. The following day, me and June had been ice-skating and when i went in the house, Norma said 'You've had a visitor today', "who, me"? 'But i told whoever it was that you will be back about six', so make sure yer stay in, but she wasn't giving anything away, was it a he or a she? 'Yer will av ter wait and see', won't yer,' then i caught the sly wink she gave mam.

Who-ever it was, she said would be back at six o'clock,' bloody hell!, 'it's half five now, and i only come home early because cos my period started, and i had nothing with me. 'Well then yer better hurry up then hadn't yer', but when i asked for a clue, 'oh sod it, im going to have a wash', and Norma said' time is kicking, with that i ran up the stairs and the bath had already been filled, 'this is a bleedin wind up, i thought, anyway i was in and out by the time i counted to thirty. Spot on the dot, six o'clock, the knock came, 'il get it' i shouted, why was i shaking? I wondered, I soon found out when i opened the door, it was Alan, 'thank god your home' he said, as he put his arms round me, i have really missed you, and now at least you live nearer, il be able ter see yer when i want to,' "thats if yer still want me to! "Of course i do, yer bloody melon," i told him that i had only been home for a short time and i had left the address with my aunty Marge anyway, then we heard the shout from the living room, 'Take the poor lad in the kitchen, and make him a cup of tea,' followed by laughter. After a cup of tea, we just sat in the kitchen talking, he patted his knee, in other words, he wanted me to sit on his knee, and because i trusted him, i sat on his knee then i realised i had a sanitary towel on, and i jumped off, i felt mortified in case he noticed,! I need not have worried, i think we both understood each other, and i would have trusted him with my life at that time. He had been coming to see me every night and on a Friday, we would go skating or he would take me the flicks, but June wasn't too happy about it, she didn't want me to see him every night, she had her nose pushed out, but she had always known about Alan, i told her everything about him, and it would only be a matter of time before we met up again as i knew he would come and find me, the only thing i didn't bank on was, it was sooner than later, and anyway, if she didn't like it, then tough, because i had known him a lot longer than her.

 The house was ready for us to move into now, mam had sorted everything out, so after being at Norma's and uncle Frank's house, for just on six weeks, it felt really sad to be leaving, but we all knew it was coming, so two days later, we all said our goodbye's and tears had been shed, we set off on the Saturday morning to yet another place in the wilds, and hopefully a new start, and after asking mam if June could come, just for the weekend, we left in uncle Frank's van. We were headed for a place called HALEWOOD, a brand new council estate.

It was early on a Saturday morning, and when we finally got to the place where we were gonna live, it was all fields and just one long road, that never seemed to end, we got to another road called BARNCROFT ROAD and they still hadn't finished building, there was only three houses that had anyone living in them, we would be the fourth, another bloody maisonette but more modern, at least that was something i suppose, but we couldn't even get to the door because it was all soil, not even a path, so uncle Frank went to see the blokes that were doing the building and asked them for some paving stones, then with the help of one of them, they made a makeshift path, better than nothing i suppose. Even before we got to the front door, mam bellowed', 'shoes off all of yer' 'yer not bleeding going in there with shoes on', 'Oh bleedin ell mam, why all the fuss? We all found out why when she opened the front door, "What the"!, we were all gobsmacked, we had never seen a more lovely sight, it had fitted carpet right through and all the same pattern, even up the stairs, and the bathroom and toilet and the three bedrooms, everything was brand new, till someone piped out, 'Aye mam, there's no beds', 'Oh their gettin delivered this afternoon with the rest of the stuff,' 'so we can't do much till they come' just let's get cracking and put what stuff we have got, and put everything where it should go'. Even all the stuff we had to put away was all new, right down to a knife and fork. The big van pulled up, and we all waited with baited breath as two men started to unload it, there were a bed each, a bigger one for mum, because she would be having a cot in with her for Carol, who was still a baby at that time.

Then along came boxes full of brand new bedding and towels, and finally wardrobes for each bedroom. Mother had really excelled herself this time, well she had the money to do it, so father served a purpose after all.

Mam shouted, 'take all them upstairs and make the beds, and put everything yer don't need in the cupboard on the landing,' 'Are aye mam, me and teresa moaned,' 'oh fuckin ell, all of yer make yer bleedin own', I never said no more, i got June to help me, then we heard a shout to go and get our dinner, we had never had a dinner off mam before, but then, she had never been loaded before.

Everything you needed, from bread to a box of matches, i wanted to pinch my-self to make sure i wasn't dreaming, because i wanted to savour the taste, but it was real, so after me and June had finished, we went to the end of the path, and sat on the little fence that separated the houses, and we were just talkin when a blue mini pulled into the road, we just stared at it, then when it got closer, i realised it was Alan and a friend, who brought him up to see me, i jumped off the gate, and ran towards him, miserable arse June just stayed were she was, 'stupid cow' i thought, i couldn't contain my joy, 'it's Alan, it's Alan i shouted', he jumped out of the passenger seat, and rushed toward me, mam knew we were boyfriend and girlfriend, but she liked Alan because she was a friend of his mum, 'what are you doing here? I said, 'i had ter come and see my favourite girl didn't i, anyway il be comin up on me bike, so i had to find the way, anyway now i know, but sorry babe, it can't be every night because of work, but at least it's not as far as bloody Birmingham,! Don't i get a kiss, and i could feel my face going bright red as he grabbed hold of my face, he knew i was embarrassed which made him laugh, the git, so he did it all the more, till i belted him in the belly. June still hadn't moved, 'Come on, let's go for a ride around this place,' whats up with yer mate? 'Oh don't take any notice of her', she just wants it to be me an her, she's not keen on lads, 'I hope you're not either, only this one here, he said pointing to himself and pulling me closer,' stop it you, me mam might see, i said, well, she knows im yer boyfriend so whats the problem?.

I know i have said i never knew about love, or what a girlfriend is supposed to know about, but i secretly felt what i thought was love for Alan, and he knew it, so the crafty sod had brought a friend to match-make June and his friend, but June was having none of it. 'I shouted to mam that we were going for a drive round, and all i heard was 'don't be long' don't forget June has got to get the six o'clock bus at the top', ok i said and then i had to struggle to get June into the car, but not for long.

'What did yer say that for madam"? Alan said, There's sod all round here, we were gonna go to a cafe or somewhere, Alan said, but before i could say anything, June wanted to stop the car, 'just stop the car now, she demanded! 'Who the fuck did she think she was, given bleedin orders, the cheeky cow, but Alan's mate who by then i knew his name was Dave, carried on driving and i told June to stop moaning, and we wouldn't be long anyway, but they could both see she meant it, so because she was a selfish bitch, we stopped in the middle of no-were and she jumped out and started running, without a clue where she was going, there was nowhere to go.

Now i was getting mad, i told Alan to hang on while i ran after her, otherwise, she would have got lost. She heard me running after her and shouting her, but she still ran, and Alan and Dave were right behind us, for a while, and when she saw them, she dodged down some other road full of big posh houses, and hid behind one of them. Meanwhile, Dave had given up and they drove off, without a word from Alan, they just went. I shouted after them, they must have heard me, but they carried on until they were out of site. I called June every name under the sun, i was fuckin fuming with her,' when she knew they had gone, she came from behind some big garden and i told her, 'You can fuck off now, after that, see what yer fuckin done, yer fuckin bitch! 'But i didn't give her the chance to speak'. 'There's the bus stop there, so yer might as well wait here, cos your not comin with me, an don't fuckin worry about yer nightdress, cos its goin in the fuckin bin, then i walked away and left her standing by the bus stop, and that was the last time i ever saw her, two weeks later, mam said she had been killed in a car accident, she had read about it in the paper!

That was the moment i realised that i did love Alan, well, they would call it puppy love today, and it hurt, it really did, because for weeks after, i tried and tried, to get him on the phone at work but he only answered a couple of times, then after that, he had told his boss not to accept any more calls from me. There was one more chance for me to see him, and that chance came when i was babysitting for his aunty Marlene, who was now living in CHILDWALL, an estate not too far from where i lived, i had managed to get hold of him and he knew were i was, so i told him if he didn't come and let me explain, then i would go, and leave the kids on their own, which i never would have done, but it was the only way i could get him there, and i waited and waited until i heard the motorbike pull up and stop. He never said a word, he just stood by the window, and he seemed so cold to-ward me, like he didn't want to listen to anything i had to say, 'Why didn't you stop your mate? I asked, "Why, so you could make an even more fool out of me than you already did? 'I did wave for you to wait' it wasn't my fault, an she's dead now, i tried and cried till in the end, i told him to go, which he did, i made myself believe that if his pride would let him leave me, then i couldn't have meant that much to him, he said i had hurt him, but he would never know how much he had hurt me, because i would never see him again. It was years later, after i had seen the death of his mum, who he doted on, that i phoned his aunty, and asked her if he was ok, she told me he was married then with three kids, and to this day, i think and wonder if we would have still been together, but no, he was too vain, and i wouldn't have the best husband in the world for over forty years and five lovely kids of my own, i told my husband about Alan, but did i love him? No, i said goodbye to that part of my life when he put his pride before his feelings, so once again, GOODBYE ALAN GALLAGHER!

After that night, i wouldn't speak to anyone, just cried all the time for over a week, and i certainly never took any notice to mam, when she told me to buck my idea's up, because my school work was suffering, i didn't care, when mam had told me about June, she expected me to cry, and she got right in my face because i didn't, 'Why should i care what happend to her, i said'. It's that bastard's fault anyway, and then i felt an almighty slap across my face of f mam, 'Don't ever let me hear you swear like that again', said mam, not realising i had said it out loud, but i roared back at her 'Why not?, you do it all the time, then i got another slap and then sent to bed, 'yer only fourteen, it's only a lad, fer god's sake,!'Was my dad "only a lad once? Then she came toward me and i had to leg it up the stairs, because if she had anything in her hand, you could guarantee she would launch it at you.

When i got inside my room, or rather mine and Teresa's, because we had to share, I thought how could i be such a heartless bitch about June, and yet still i couldn't forget what she did.

At the age of fourteen, if you had a job, they would let you leave school, if you had proof of a job, but although i didn't know this, for the simple truth was that i was never in school anyway, always bunking off, it was a girl could leave,' but not before she said. I was over the moon, so i set about looking for a job, and found one, just across the big field at the back of where we lived, so on my last day at school, as i walked out of the gates, i took everything that concerned school, i ripped everything up and shouted with glee as i threw the lot over the fence.

PART ELEVEN

MY FIRST JOB

When i got my first job, i was over the moon, it was everything i had always wanted to do, and i was getting paid to do something that i really wanted to do when as a young girl, but never thought i would because i was told i would need to train for me to do it, well that put an end to that dream, because of my lack of schooling, was bad, as im sure you can tell, because for one, i can't spell to save my life, so what you see is what you get, but anyway i went after the job anyway, and i got it, i couldn't believe it, i was to start on the following Monday.

At the time, the place was called, The Horses Rest, where old horses that had seen most of their working lives as work-horses, or farm horses that would pull heavy farm machinery across very wide fields, could no longer do the work, they were sent here to live out the rest of their lives at leisure.

When i got to The Horses Rest on my starting day, i couldn't wait to start, but i was amazed to find out it wasn't just horses that were kept there, there was all kinds of animals there, mainly cats and dogs, but rabbits and other things. I was in my dream job, and i didn't care what i had to do, i loved caring for the animals and nothing else mattered. I had to be in the kennels by eight o'clock every morning, but i only had to walk over the field in every morning, was to clean all the caged animals first, but as the dogs got used to me, they used to howl every time they saw me, so if no-one was looking, i would let them have the run of the kennels, till it was time to feed them and they loved it, well wouldn't you after being stuck in a cage all night?

My other jobs included cleaning every cage, and wash them all out with disinfectant one by one, but i enjoyed it, and the best was taking the dogs on walks one by one, it was like i was getting to know them, and them me, and they looked forward to their walks, and at night when i turned the lights off, they would howl and i could still hear them when i was half way across the field going home.

One day i went into work, i saw this notice on the wall, saying that the RSPCA were taking over the Horses Rest, but there would be no other changes, except that any dogs or strays, would only be kept for seven days,

Then, if it wasn't claimed or found a home, then they had to be destroyed, the cruel bastards i said. When i went to make a start on the cages, there were little cards that where pre-dated and when i asked what they were for, i was told that was the date they would be put down, that was when i noticed Monty on a lead with another carer, 'Where's Monty going ? i asked, it's his seventh day, i was told,! 'Oh no its not', il take him home with me later, just leave him in his cage till i go home'. 'You just can't take him, you need to have permission, so i asked if i could run home and get a note of my mother, 'Ok, but don't be long, i was gone before she could finish what she was saying. To say mam was not pleased was an understatement, 'il find him a home later, please mam i pleaded, just till i get home, 'Make fuckin sure yer do', 'im not avin no bleedin dog messing my house up'. Monty ended up staying with us for six months, till he died of old age, i was broken-hearted, but that didn't stop me taking other dogs home, which i did manage to re-home, that was till i took a big sheep dog called Pip home. He had been there two days and on the third day, i went out the back garden to peg some washing on the line, and because i wouldn't let him in the back, he jumped out the bleedin window, i mean jumped, right through the glass, then he had to go, but he ended up back where he had come from, but every time he was due to be put to sleep, i would change the dates on the cards, till one day when i was told to go with one of the head carer's, and what i saw made me throw up, he put pip in a iron like cage, then attached wires to each ear, then he threw a bucket of water over him, then he flicked a switch on the wall, and then i realised he was putting pip down, i run out the room, with pip's screams ringing in my ears, he had electrocuted pip, and it was barbaric the way they did it, they then sacked me, because i wouldn't do the same to another dog,! 'I told them to fuck off, i went there to help animals, not kill them, and to this day, i can't watch any advertisements done by the RSPCA, or anything concerning cruelty to any animal, because it really upsets me, so that was the end of my dream job.

Mam was made up that i lost my job, if it had been any other job, she would have hit the bleedin roof. In the sixties, you could walk out of one job, then get another with-in an hour or less, so i got a job in a place called BARE BRAND, where they made nylon stockings and tights, when they came into fashion. They had very strict when you started, and a manicure every day before you started work, and another in the afternoon, so it got on your nerves a bit, because you were on piece-work, which was you only got payed for the amount of work you did, and if you weren't that fast, you would only pick up button's for wages, then on the other hand, when you had gained the experience to be as fast as everybody else, thats when you would see the difference in your wages, and you would welcome a bit of time away from your machine, getting a manicure, and feel pampered. It was a very detailed job, but rewarding when you got the knack.

I made quite a few friends at my job, and at the ripe old age of fifteen, i started to drink, so, on a Thursday when we got paid, we would go to a pub called THE ELEPHANT, in the nearby, WOOLTON village, and no-one questioned our age, because we worked at the local factory. There was one girl in particular, her name was Pam Smith, she lived at the top of our road, ROSEHEATH DRIVE, and right facing a pub, called the HALE-FELLOW.

We became good friends over the time we worked together, in and out of work, we would go everywhere together, and we were always in and out of each other's houses, and would take turns in whose house when we had sleep over's. Teresa had left home at this point, having gotten to know a bloke mam didn't like, so she moved out, but not before he gave mam some of what Teresa was in store for. While she still lived at home, the bloke she was seeing had just come out of the Army. He would take her out, then they would end up arguing, that's when he would show his true colours, he would openly slag Teresa in front of mam, even hit her until mam decided to interfere, then he would hit mam, and start smashing the place up. This went on for a while, until mam decided enough was enough, and she was scared of him, especially when he had been drinking, because that was when he would start, so she got him arrested, and he swore he would make her pay.

She was really scared of him, and she had reason to be, because he had gave mam a hiding she wouldn't forget, plus the odd black eye, here and there, so she told Teresa to move out, because she still insisted she wanted to be with him, and he never changed, but mam never spoke to Teresa for nearly fourteen years, and that was that, she was never spoken about, it was as though she didn't exist, and at that time i didn't care, cos we were never that close anyway, so why should i care about her, the only good thing i thought at that particular time, was i gained a little respect for mam, why it took so long il never know. From then on, we seemed to get on a bit better, and i started to call her mum, and even she noticed that i called her mum, cos she said in her normal tone, that i was allowed to do whatever i wanted. It was my turn to stay at Pam's, and i never had the heart to tell her, i didn't like staying, because there would be three of us having to sleep in the same bed, and i was used to having my own bed, all to myself, and Pam's sister Rosie would be in with me and Pam when i was stayed, only because her mother was always pissed, and she was prone to bring men back to sleep, but it would depend who the lucky one was, and who would buy her the most drinks, but she was known to have a bad reputation!

We used to try a different pub every week, one week it would be, The Hunts-Cross and then The Hill Foot, then my mum had found out, and that was the end of that friend-ship, and since i didn't know anyone as good or as long as i knew Pam, i stopped going out, and just hung around the area, with other girls and lads. When i was sixteen, mum said i could have a party with just a few of the boys and girls, mum said it was ok, as long as there was no damage or mess, and it had to end at ten o'clock, i was made up. Mum had been going to a club for a couple of months called the Devonshire, down by SEFTON PARK, where she would have a good time, mum never give a shit, Why should she? Dad had been dead for only two years, but that never stopped her, that was when the thought struck, she was doing the same thing that Pam's mum was doing, the only difference was that she never brought any men home, but give it time! . . . Her excuse, she was still young enough to have boyfriends, so when she started to bring men home, she was doing exactly the same thing pam's mum, and for that she made me give up a good friend, fuckin hypocrite. There was one in particular whose name was Stan, who seemed to be the flavour of the month at that time, and he thought he was bleedin God's gift to women.

The day of my sixteenth birthday arrived, and mum was getting ready to go out, and although she had already told me that we could only have shandy, as if i thought, she already knew i went out to pubs with Pam, and i was working, but shandy, no chance. As she went out the front door, my mates came in the back way, complete with cider and port and a few records, then the party started, with food laid on of course. Everything was going well, having a drink and dancing, when suddenly the front door was kicked in, and mum came running in, her nose and mouth, pouring with blood, she ran right up the stairs to the bathroom and locked herself in.

I was going to see what was wrong, when a big scrawny hand pushed me out the way, nearly falling down the stairs, 'What the fuck have you done to my mum? I said to him, he took no notice, and put his foot through the door, 'Margaret, get the police mum shouted! But i never got the chance, he came down the stairs after me, and to me 'Get this fuckin lot out of here, he roared, meaning my mates, then he turned on me, smacking me so hard, i smashed my head on the corner of the door, the next thing i knew, all my mates were gone, and there was blood everywhere, i was crying when mum came down, 'Whats that cut on her head? 'You bastard,' no-one hits my kids, she told him to fuck off and stay away from the house. 'He's just made a holy show of me,' that bastard,' and i ended up with six stitches, i don't think i'll forget that birthday in a hurry.

Anyone and everyone who knew me, heard about my so-called party, but for all the wrong reasons, and i was the talk of the youth club i used to go to, which was a disused football changing room, i remember my sister Teresa used to go there before i even started to go, but when i started going, she would crack on she never knew me, and because i couldn't dance to save my life, i asked her would she teach me some of the steps that where in fashion at the time, i was told to fuckin drop dead, 'sorry to disappoint you bitch', but im still very much alive', i told her some time later. As my friends started to change, so did i, had met a lad called Tony Carroll, who lived over the other side of the estate, we started out as mates, then we became boyfriend/girlfriend. There were about ten of us, all 'couples' and we would just hang about together in the village. As we grew closer within the group, we would do stupid games and competitions like a certain dares, Then, i thought i was too old for games and also ended the boyfriend/girlfriend thing as well with Tony. We all went our separate ways, but we always remained friends, even in our adult days, when we all had our own kids and had settled down, even now over nearly forty years, the lad who was the very first boy, sort of boyfriend when we lived in the dingle, he lives right facing me, in Runcorn, i get on well with his wife and his daughter as it turned out, was a girlfriend of my son, James, i really thought it was weird, anyway back to Halewood, i was at home one day, when mum got a phone call from uncle George's wife, Ann, 'i couldn't believe we had our own phone then', anyway Ann was asking mum if she could borrow mum's wedding ring, because she had pawned her own, and didn't have the money to redeem it, she could only pay the interest that meant they would keep it until she was able to get her ring back, and uncle George had asked her where her wedding ring was a couple of times but she was scared now, in case he found out. I told mum that she had already borrowed a ring off the woman who owned the corner shop, and she asked me how i knew, and i told her, that i was the one who took the letter over to her, and she gave Ann an old ring she had, and told her not to worry, and to pass it back when she got sorted, thats how i knew. 'Well, she must have gave it back, or she wouldn't ask', mum said, but i reminded her about how devious Ann was, so she had been warned, but she sent it to her anyway. Two months later, mum got another phone call, but this time it was Uncle George to tell mum that his wife Ann had passed away the day before, they had told him she had a cancerous tumour, but never knew. As i caught the word cancer, i was half way down the stairs, then i found mum in tears sitting on the bottom stair, as she told uncle George that she would be in Birmingham the next day, with the rest of their family. She told me after the funeral, that she asked George if she could have Ann's wedding ring as a momentum only to be told that she didn't have one, she must have sold it, he said, like everything else, the only one that she had was the one she had been given by the woman from the corner shop who didn't want it back, so mum had to take it, she didn't want to tell him that his wife had borrowed her wedding ring, but she had no way of getting it back now.

It was also known then, when all the family were together, that Ann had also borrowed Aunty Norma's ring, which she never got back either, and when she had told uncle Frank, he hit the bleeding roof, she said but rather than upset his brother, he said nothing, he just bought her another one, but it wasn't the same, the one she had lost had taken all the memories and sentiment with it, and upset her deeply.

I was a few months away from my birthday, soon i would be seventeen, when mum had heard that Teresa was living with her boyfriend's parents, which made her mad, 'She's made her own fuckin bed', and him!, that bastard should be fuckin locked away fer good', cos he won't stop knocking her about, he's a twat and he'll never change, he's a fuckin lunatic and if that's what she wants, then she can get on with it'! I was seeing a lad called Mick Morrell, he lived in the big posh houses near the village, and he drove round on a scooter, which was what attracted me, cos it certainly wasn't him, he was a proper mummy's boy. He was an only child and his mum would try and push us together, at every opportunity, she would do her best to make sure we were left on our own, even made sure i was asked to 'Sunday afternoon tea' which would consist of ham and cheese sandwich, chocolate cake, and pop, which i thought was odd, no 'tea'. 'Go into the parlour and watch television' she would say' 'she's fuckin gone with the fairy's' i thought, 'so is he, so i left and that was the last i saw of him.

I had met a girl called Sandra, who lived just around the corner from us, in Hornbeam Road, and we started to go out a couple of nights a week, when we heard of a club just opened in Widnes, quite a bus ride away, but the group we both liked was playing there at that weekend, and we really wanted to see them, we heard them on the radio all the time at work, so we had the chance to see them, live, at the QUEENS HALL in Widnes, so we decided to go, i couldn't wait, THE ROCKIN BERRYS they were called, and all that week, time dragged.

PART TWELVE

"WHY"

The day of the concert had arrived and we couldn't wait, there was only the two of us going, just me and Sandra Holmes, who was my best friend at the time. It was coming up to the end of January, and it was freezing, and we had to queue up for nearly two hours, but it was worth it, to see my favourite group at that time, i had been excited all day, and now we were finally there. When we got inside, the first place we made for, was of course the bar, we each got a glass of lager, and a vodka and lime, and i could see the bloke looking at me, but he must have thought i was old enough, so he served us, i was going to be eighteen that year, and they never used to ask for I.D. then, so we went to find a table, when Sandra said, 'Don't forget the last bus is at eleven,' so we'l have to leave about ten to'. 'Bloody hell, san, wev'e only just got our first drink and your talkin about the last bus, don't worry, we won't miss it, i said. 'I don't like this drink, meaning the vodka, so i asked her if she wanted it, and she could buy me a port and lemon, she agreed then went to the bar, while i watched the table and our bag's, it was really crowded now, so you didn't take any chances, so i waited for her to come back, when i noticed this bloke coming toward me, not taking any notice as he got nearer, i thought he was going to the bar, but he stopped by me, and i froze, i didn't feel comfortable being there on my own, and i kept looking to see where she was, but when i looked up at the bar, Sandra was still in the queue, bleedin hell, i was shitting myself now, then i heard, it again, 'I said, can i get you a drink! I just said, im waiting for my friend, she's at the bar now, but thanks anyway, and he walked away. 'Thank fuck for that,' i thought to myself and was relieved to see Sandra on her way over,

Finally, The Rocking Berries came on, and with our bags at our feet, we danced and danced, until the prick who had hounded me suddenly pushed Sandra away and he said, 'fuck of you; to her, 'she's dancing with me now', i told him to get lost, but Sandra just walked away, and that was it, i was stuck with him, and right then, i was petrified to say anything to him, but it didn't stop me thinking, what the fuck was i gonna do now, he really scared me, i was looking everywhere for Sandra, then i spotted her heading for the cloakroom, and when i shouted her, she completely just blanked me out, 'you fuckin bitch' i thought to myself, now i was on my own, i just as i was getting to the bus stop, i saw my last bus leave, but the driver saw me, and when i thought he was gonna stop, he smirked at me and carried on driving, i just stuck two fingers up to him and he burst out laughing, bastard. To say i was scared, was an understatement, i was petrified, and crying, i couldn't even afford a taxi and it was pitch black. I started to walk, until i felt this tap on my shoulder, 'Whats up'? i turned round with fright, because i jumped back and there he was, the lad from the dance floor. 'I started to run, and he just grabbed me, 'Calm down he kept saying', but he wouldn't leave me alone, and me being the thick shit that i was then, i believed him, when he told me that he could get me a lift, if i would just stop running.

He had taken me, to his "sisters" house, so he said, and when we stopped at a house in darkness, i asked 'Where are we? Then he told me it was too late to go to his sisters, so he took me to his home, i turned to walk away, 'Well, it's too late to walk all that way, he said 'How the fuckin hell do you know where i live, i shouted, i had no sooner said the words, when he put his hand over my mouth, and dragged me to a bedroom, that i found out later, was a room, at the back of the living room, he flung me down onto a bed, while he still had his hand over me, then he heard footsteps coming down stairs, so he put me face down onto a pillow, then he lay on top of me, so it looked as though there was only one body lying there, 'Don't dare open your mouth, or your dead! . . . Those words still haunt me, as i write this, i am reliving the moment he then raped me,! He then made me walk, till he was out of sight, then i ran to the nearest house in tears, the poor old woman, god help her, got the shock of her life, when she saw the state i was in, and she asked if i wanted her to phone the police, and i said yes please. That lady sat with me till daylight, she even stayed with me, all the time the police were asking me questions, most of which i couldn't answer, because i knew nothing, but there was one thing that stood out, i said, 'He had a star tattoo, on his forehead, and from that little bit of information, they knew who he was, and i was to find out then who it was that raped me. His name, i would not ever be able to forget, but he was, and yes, i am glad to say "was" because he's dead, he died twelve months after he raped me, so good riddance, the evil piece of shit, but that wasn't the last i was to hear from him, only i never knew it then . . .

At last, i was taken home by the police, but i asked them to drop me off at the corner, because i wasn't in the mood for one of mums lecture's, all i wanted to do was sleep, but she would see me covered in bruises anyway, so i tried to sneak in, should be ok, i thought, it was only seven o'clock, she'll still be asleep, the lecture could wait, but when i looked behind me, the policeman that brought me home, was walking up the path, then without a word, he banged loudly, and i could hear mum swearing, and moaning, "now im gonna get it', thanks . . .

The policeman told mum everything that had happend, but as soon as he left, mum just told me to get a bath, then she went back to bed, no interest in how i was, or how i felt, she just said 'don't wake the others up', charming, 'she didn't give a shit' pure and simple, well about me, she never. And god help the so-called friend, Sandra, called herself a mate! I had better mates in the dog Kennels, i could have been murdered for all she cared. After mum had gone back to bed, i had a bath, then a s i went to the kitchen to make myself a cup of chocolate, i glanced out of the window, and i got the shock of my bleedin life, i was so scared, i had to look twice, just to make sure, but i looked again, the horror of the night before was before me, he stood right outside our gate, and stood there, making gesture's to me with his hands, i just froze. I went to the door, armed with an empty milk bottle, and then he was gone! 'Where the fuck' my words froze into air, i never imagined him, he was there, now he had gone . . . . My mum came running down the stairs, 'what the bleeding hell's goin on,? She roared

'How did he know where yer lived? Mum asked, 'I don't bleedin know, i don't even know him, don't even know how he got here, cos the police brought me home,' 'you saw them yourself, im scared, i said. 'Get ter bed fer a couple of hour's, it's your turn to do the brushing to-day'. She's on another planet her, what kind of mother worries about brushing the bleedin carpet above a daughter being raped, certainly not mine.

It was while i was brushing the stairs, that mum noticed i had blood on my legs, only then did she show concern and sent me to bed, with a hot water bottle for my sore stomach, and something i never argued about.

The following morning, i had to do my share of everything, and mum had never been very house-proud until we moved to this place, but i could understand her wanting it nice, but she had a fetish about her carpets, they had to be brushed every day, from top to bottom, with a farting little hand-brush. It was three days later, i was to come face to face with the bastard that raped me, i was getting off the bus, coming home from work, and there he was, just sitting there, on the wall. I stopped dead in my tracks, and panicked, but the only thing he said to me was, 'See how easy i can find you! My blood ran cold, 'Just dare tell anyone, and you'll be sorry! That was to be the start of my night-mare.

MY NIGHT-MARE BEGINS!

PART ONE

MARCH 1967

I was now working in a place called TRARMERS, in between Speak and Halewood, we did packing of anything really, from glass jars to anything that was classed as 'toiletries' really, it wasn't as good as my last job, at the stocking factory, money wise, but it wasn't as boring, at least they played a radio over loud speakers, and you could smoke on 'the job', so you never had to keep leaving your work when you wanted a smoke, plus you could get a cup of tea, or a drink when you wanted. That weekend, i was now buddies again with Pam Smith, having dumped the other so-called mate, Sandra Holmes, but not befor i gave her a gob full, anyway, as i said it was just me and Pam now, and we had been out over the week-end, and now i was paying the price for drinking too much, my head was banging and i felt really sick. When mum shouted me on the Monday morning for work, i only got as far as getting my legs out of the bed, when i fell back down, and the room was spinning, i was sat on the bed, throwing up, when mum told me that i had been doing it all night, but i didn't remember, but i did see the bucket at the side of the bed, 'You can't go ter work like that', mum said, 'and don't think yer paying me any less,' 'its yer own bleedin fault,' She was all heart, only ever worried about money. As the day turned into night, i was still throwing up, mum said' Yer must av ad a bad bottle of whatever it is that yer were drinking,' but i only drank cider, i told her, 'well then, yer better get yerself over to the doctor's in the morning' 'cos yer might need a sick note fer work', mum said. 'I'll make an appointment fer yer', with that she walked out the door. Our doctor at that time, was a DR GATLEY, and he was only across the road, by the bus stop, anyway mum said she had got me in to see him that afternoon, and as soon as i walked in the doctor's room, he called for the nurse to come in, because he wanted to examine me, and he had to have a female in with him while he did this, and all this was weird, because i hadn't even told him why i was there, so why all the fuss.

'I understand from your mother,' that you have been throwing up the last few days,' he said! 'Yes, i told him, mum thinks i must have had a bad drink, i told him, but i wasn't prepared for what came next. "Oh She knows whats wrong with you, he said while he examined me, and i can confirm that you are seven to eight weeks pregnant, and then after he done some maths in his head, 'you should have your baby around the ninth of October . . . . I was struck dumb, 'im not Pregnant' i told him' i can't be, cos i haven't had sex with anyone,' i haven't, then the bomb hit me, the rape, 'Oh my god, the rape', as i started to worry how to tell mum, the doctor read my thoughts, 'don't worry about your mother,' 'she already knows! That conniving bitch, i thought, no bleedin wonder she couldn't wait for me to get the doctors.

Mum was brushing the top of the stairs when i walked in, 'Well', she said, 'He said you already know, i said crying at the same time, "You're gonna marry him or get rid of it"! I couldn't believe what i was hearing! As I was walking home, in total shock, me, having a baby, im only bloody seventeen for god's sake, I can't have a baby, I just can't, and i couldn't believe my ear's when my mum's word's echoed in my head.

"Mum," 'No' I can't marry that bastard, and i don't want to! 'How could you say that, when you know what he did to me, and i won't get rid of it, "You're only worried about the fuckin neighbours", i said, but you don't give a give a shit about me, then again, you never did! I told her i was moving out, 'aunty Tre will help me, and it won't finish up in a bucket like i was supposed to, so fuck you, then i ran up the stairs to get my stuff, when she ran after me with the poker, 'again' so i had to lock myself in the bathroom, till both of us calmed down, because the mood she was in, she would have battered the baby out of me. I knew she would never change, i had been a fool to try and work things out, but by me giving her some respect, she saw that as a red rag to a bull, well now the respect went out the window, from then on, i hated her.

As two hours had past, i was wondering why things where so quiet, so i sneaked down the stairs, having made sure the living room door was shut, when all of a sudden i threw up, all over her lovely carpet, and my bag fell against the door, but mum came from the kitchen, not the living room as i expected. 'Where are you going?' she said, 'you can't go anywhere like that, come in here and i'll make you something to settle your stomach.

Whats she up to now, i thought, but as i walked in the kitchen, Mrs Murphy our next door neighbour was sitting there, drinking tea, 'come here love' she said, sit here with me till yer mum makes yer something to drink, no wonder mum was being nice i thought. Mum had made some porridge and told me it would put the lining back on my stomach, then when i had that, she told me to go and lay down on the couch, with a blanket over me, 'Oh i wasn't fooled for one minute,' this was all for Mrs Murphy's benefit, thats what the kindness was all about. Mum must have told her what was wrong, but i wasn't sure if she told her the full story, so i said nothing. The porridge never stayed down long, mum had to rush upstairs to get the bucket, in case i was sick again, in her precious living room, so i had been palmed off on the couch for the night, 'just in case' mum said.

I must have dozed off, because all i remember was mum and Mrs Murphy came in the living room just as i woke, they had come in to watch the telly, 'Coronation Street was just starting, and they wanted to watch it, so i told mum that i wanted the toilet, as i eased my way up from the couch, 'Do yer want me ter come with yer? I just looked at her and said no, i'll be ok i said. The only reason i wanted to go upstairs for a ciggie, so i would open the toilet window, and blow the smoke out. The ciggie made me sick again, so i flushed it down the toilet and went back downstairs, back to the couch. It was then Mrs Murphy came over and put her arms around me, i started to cry again, 'Don't worry love, you're not the first and you won't be the last'! I never knew how often i worry about that now, 'but mum, i don't want to marry him, he's already said he's gonna kill me if i told anyone, please don't make me, and i don't want to get rid of it, because iv' heard people die when they have that done'. Mrs Murphy must have had words with my mum, because she asked me what he looked like, i had almost forgot, but all i could remember was he always seemed to wear a cream coloured suit, and the thing that stood out the most, was the tattoo of a star in the middle of his forehead, when mum said 'how do you know he always a cream suit,?' have you seen him again?, so i told her about him hanging round, even at the bus stop when i got home from work, i told her', and he always had the same suit on.! Nothing more was said after that, and i never went back to work after that day. But the next day, the cheeky bastard went round the back way, and knocked on the back door, so i shouted mum, who then came running in with Mrs Murphy, who had just walked in, 'whats the matter, whats up? I pointed out the window to show her who was standing there, 'Is that him? She asked, and i just nodded. No one was more shocked than me, when she let him in, i ran to Mrs Murphy who said 'Mary, what are yer doing? I was petrified, and i was clinging on to her while mum was asking him what he wanted, i couldn't believe what i was hearing. "I've just heard that she's pregnant', Is it true?

I couldn't believe what i was hearing, Mum asking him, what he wanted, 'Well if it's true,' I have a right to know, and I will marry her! 'Do you want to marry him?' mum said to me, 'Mum, do you really have to ask? I don't want to marry that piece of shit, i don't even know him, and that bastard raped me! 'Fuckin get out; NOW, i roared, as i pushed him toward the back door where he came in, as he left, i ran to the kitchen and picked up a bottle of milk, which was the nearest, and i ran to the front door just as he came through the block, and i threw it at him, sadly missing him, but i shouted 'Don't fuckin come near me again, or the police will be here!

Mrs Murphy led me to the living room, because i was crying, 'Here yer go girl, a nice cup of sweet tea,' it's good for shock. Mum had been over the road, to clear the broken bottle and glass that i had thrown, and the first thing she did was give me a slap, right across the face, 'Don't ever let me hear you swear again she said,' Well i had a bleedin good teacher didn't i! She came toward me again, only Mrs Murphy stopped her, 'Mary, the poor kid is scared enough, 'leave her for a while to calm down.'

I took my cup of tea, up to my bedroom, mainly so i could have a smoke, because i was shaking, when mum caught me leaning out the window, 'Oh god, here we go again, but i was wrong, 'Why are yer sneaking, i' have known for ages that your smoking,' so you may as well do it in front of me,' i was gobsmacked, i wasn't was tempted to ask, if i could have some of what she was on, because you couldn't know what mood she was going to be in the next ten minutes. Well at least i didn't have to hide my smoking anymore, the only problem was that she must have clocked me, pinching the odd ciggie, when she left hers lying about, but she threw me a pack of Woodbines, and said, 'Here, smoke yer bleedin own'. Oh happy days, i thought, she must have read my mind. The only downfall of my being pregnant, was that all my clothes were all too small, so mum and Mrs M now, as she told me to call her, had got together and come up with an assortment of stuff i could wear, 'just till the baby is born', there were tops that they called smocks, trousers, which were not too bad, but the coat they came up with made me cringe, Jesus, im not wearing that, i thought, but because it was getting colder and nearing my time, it was wear it, or stay in, and i would have chose to stay in, but that wasn't an option, as i had to go the doctors and there were hospital visits as well, which i hated. I was booked into Liverpool Maternity Hospital, which itself was ok, but i didn't like the clinic, because when they called your name, they always called you mrs, but it seemed to only happen when i went, they would call Miss M O'PREY, then everyone would turn and look at who it was, because it was a stigma, that you were not married. It was only once a month i had to go there, but now as i was only four weeks away from my due date, i had to go every week. Mrs M had been busy knitting away for ages and mum had been buying little things each week, like little vests, and little white night-gowns, the main thing was the big pram she had paid for, i was over the moon with it, and it acted as a cot at night, all you had to do was lift the top off. One week, mum brought me some knickers, 'Bloody hell mum, their like tents, i said, but when i tried them on they were quite comfy, over my big belly, which i was convinced was going to burst because it was massive. As time got closer, i was petrified, not knowing what to expect, but mum kept her mouth shut except to say i would be ok. She must love me after all, so i thought.

The day arrived, when i had to go into hospital, to be started off the next morning, and i couldn't stop shaking, the tea Mrs M had made me, i only felt some relief when i wished that bastard who had put me in that state in the first place was in hell. I started crying, when it was time to leave, 'Come on, will yer, fer Jesus sake,' said mum, she had no sympathy for me at all, 'This time tomorrow, it will all be over! When we got there, it was afternoon visiting time, so mum sat with me for all of ten minutes, time enough to have a ciggie, which was allowed then, even when you had your baby with you on the ward, you were allowed to smoke, even while you fed the baby, you were allowed to smoke, they even supplied the ash-trays, and you would also get a full breakfast. It was different standards then, not a bit like to-days standards.

When the sister came in to see me, mum was asked to leave for five minutes, just while they done their tests, then she could come back in, but when they went to find her, she had gone, 'the fuckin bitch' i said to myself.

The reason they asked her to leave, was so they could Break my 'waters', but i didn't know that, but fuckin mother did, thats why she got up and left, plus she didn't want to hear my cry, because it hurt. As the rest of the day progressed, so did my labour pains, and i was terrified, i felt as though my insides were being pulled out, and because i was crying, they pulled the curtains around me, because i was upsetting the other patients and their visitors, 'Fuck the other patients', i said! It was six thirty, before mum showed her face, she saw me in agony, she just dropped off a bottle of juice and some fruit, and without a word, she had left.

As the pain got worse, i got more scared, and scared. How? Could any woman, who called herself a mother, leave their daughter to go through childbirth alone is beyond me, because i have only one daughter, and we are so close, that when she hurts, so do i. I could not believe she did that, so to me, she wasn't a mother, not to me anyway. But i had always told everyone, 'i might forgive but i never forget! 'I can be a very good friend, but i can be a bastard of an enemy,' so what yer see is what yer get, and if you don't like it, tough! No-one will ever shit on me again, and if anyone looks side-ways at my kids, then God help them! Back to the hospital, at seven thirty am, on the 25 OCTOBER, over twenty hours of pain and fright, i had a lovely baby boy, i felt so proud that he was mine, and all traces of pain forgotten, because once you hold that precious little bundle, then all the pain is forgotten, but worth every ache and pain to follow.

I had only been back in the ward, when she walked in, beaming like a fuckin Cheshire cat, headed right for the cot, 'I'm a grandmother she said, 'Well yer certainly not a mother,' why did yer leave me on my own? No answer, just as i expected, here it comes, the excuse, 'When i phoned, they told me yer were asleep, so i didn't want to disturb yer', how kind and considerate i thought. She picked the baby up and her face lit up, 'Are you glad i didn't get rid of it now"! That got you back, you bitch! Then i felt guilty for saying it, but i didn't when i looked at her face. As i gave a quick glance over mums shoulder, 'Mum, quick get the sister! 'Why? What's up she said, following my eyes, there standing by the door in the ward, was the bastard who put me there. He just strolled over to the cot, as mum put the baby back down, he stood there looking at him, 'Well, What do you think of your son? Mum said, 'What the bleeding hell, i thought, 'Never bleeding bother asking him what he thinks, i said, Just get him out, not have a bleedin conversation with him, 'How the fuck did you know where i was anyway,? 'Someone phoned the pub last night and left a message for me he said, my temper was boiling as i roared at him. 'Just get out of here NOW, and just at that very second, our coalman at the time, Billy Lawless and his mate Jimmy, came in, and they must have heard what i said, because Billy said to him, 'You heard what she said "mate" and with that, he just turned around and walked out, and as i turned around, i saw my mother look at him and shrugged. "It was you" why? He's not having anything to do with him, 'so you can forget your neighbours, cos that's all your worried about, i'll just take him and leave if that's what you want, she was only worried about her neighbours, not her daughter. I said no more, because Billy and his mate were there, and i didn't want to spoil 'my' day. As everyone around my bed was smoking, even the ward was full of smoke, i tried to waft the smoke away, and as i did, Jimmy waved at me, which was making me laugh, i told him to stop making me laugh because it made my stitches hurt, all twelve of them, caused by me pushing, when they told me not too.

That was one day i will never forget, and would never forgive my mother for leaving me, when i needed her most, but then as usual, she had never been there for me. The nurses who looked after me knew i was by myself, so they took it in turns, to sit with me, knowing how scared i was, not knowing what to expect. May-be if she had given me some advice or told me what to expect, it might have helped a little, but right at that minute, i hated her.! She carried on being a heartless bitch, with me anyway, through the years to come, only i wasn't to know it then! I had been waiting for her to come and take me and my baby home, she was bringing some clothes for me and the baby to go home in, and i couldn't wait to show my son off. 'Come on, hurry up' i said as she walked through the door, 'I couldn't bloody help it', she said the bus was late, but we were getting a taxi home, 'oh god' im honoured, i thought.

As we made our way out of the hospital, we were headed for the bus-stop, and it was hard trying to walk because of my stitches, 'I thought we were gettin a taxi,' i asked, 'Im not fuckin made of money yer know! As we waited for the bus to come, my legs went from under me, and i fainted, right then and there. The next thing i knew, i woke up in a taxi, 'My god', it's a good job yer never had hold of the baby, she said. 'What happend? I said, feeling very sick, 'Never mind,' we're nearly home now, then yer can go ter bed, I'll look after this fella, meaning the baby." I wasn't gonna argue, because i felt lousy. When i climbed out of bed, every-where was so quiet, i thought everyone had gone out, but there was only mum and Harry in, he was made up i had a boy he said, 'now I've got a brother, and not another bloody sister, and he idolised 'him'. 'Let's call him Barry,' mum said, and for the first time, i agreed with her, he looked like a Barry i thought. Mum had already arranged to have him christened while i was still in the hospital, 'It would have been nice to have had a choice,' i said, and that's only three days away.

I never even had a choice with god-parent's, she also had that all sorted. Billy, the coalman, was his godfather, and because i could only have one godfather, his mate Jimmy, couldn't be number two, so he was called Barry-James. That was the first day of me and Jimmy as a couple.

The following Tuesday, Billy's collecting day, he came on his own, said jimmy couldn't make it, i thought 'Look out, being used again, but i was wrong, Billy asked mum if he could take me for a drink, meaning would she look after the baby, 'Yeh, go on, he's fast asleep anyway.' 'What's up Billy? 'Doesn't he want me now,' cos i have got a baby, is that it? 'Don't be silly, just sit down, i'll get the drinks. It's nothing to worry about, Billy said, he just wants me to explain things to you, before you make any decision, 'About what! I said. He then began to tell me that jimmy, was four years older than me, and that he was married, but separated a few months before he even met me, and he would understand if i didn't want any-more to do with him, or would i be willing to wait for him, till his divorce came through and thats why he never came up that night with Billy, in case i said no.

'He's been after you since before you had the baby, 'but he thought the other lad was on the scene, and when i told him he wasn't, 'he decided it was you and the baby, he wanted, and if you would wait for him. But i listened to what Billy had to say, I told Billy to tell him yes, i would wait. Then the following Friday, we went out on our first date. Jimmy spent most of our first date telling me about, how he had waited for Billy to get home, and tell him what my answer was, and when he told him i would wait, he went crazy in a made up way, and couldn't wait till he came up on the following Friday, to take me out. He took me to a pub called the Clock, just at the top off, Wavertree Road then from there we went for a meal to end the night, leaving just before the last bus home

We had been courting for four months, when we decided to tell his mum and dad, about me having a baby, and to say they were not happy about it, was a fair statement, they already knew about me, but not the baby. His mother and father told him he was making a mistake, so did his sister Joan, who never liked me from the start, but there was no love lost, because i didn't like her, she thought she was bleeding lady muck, better than anyone. She had met her to be husband, Dozy Derek, i used to call him, on a blind date set up by Jimmy, because they used to play for the same football team on a Saturday, and before Jim, had met me, he had to take her out, because she had no bloody friends of her own, she thought everyone was beneath her. Don't know why, she had the face of an imp, with a long pointy nose, she reminded me of NANNY Mc PHEE, but she was to get her pointed beak put out of joint, when one week, Jims mum and dad told me to take my baby to see them, once they knew that me and Jim were serious about staying together, Joan and Derek Service, who was then, a good mate of Jims at that time, was the bloke that was fool enough to fancy the 'witch' as i called Jims sister, had told his mother about me, already having a baby when i met her brother. One night, when we were at Jims mums house, when i had taken Barry, at his mums request, and Jims dad had him on his knee, playing with him, when i was called into the kitchen, to be told that Derek's mum had told them, that she knew me from Scotland Road, and that i had had a baby when i was fourteen, 'Well it must have happend while i was asleep', i told them, because i was still in infant school when i left Scotti Road! What that cow would have done, to split me and Jim up was beyond me, and i never spoke to her after that. 'And you, Derek Service, 'better tell your mother to get her facts right in future, or she could land herself in trouble, OK! Then because i got upset with temper, i went back and started to get Barry ready to go home, his dad asked me what was wrong, and i said 'ask your bloody daughter and her boyfriend! . . .' Then when he opened his mouth, there were apologies all round, 'Don't bother, i said to Joan,' shove it, then me and Jim got the bus back to mums. The June of 1968, the 22nd, Joan and Derek announced they were getting engaged, which was also her birthday, which was also my mother's birthday, and just to piss her off, we announced that we were getting engaged the same day, so that put some gloom on her gob, i was made up!! Four years later, i gave Jims mum and dad, their first grandchild, and a boy, at, which Stan was over the moon, we called him JAMES STANLEY, DECEMBER 21ST 1971, after Jim, and his dad, then the following April 1ST, 1972. Me and Jim were married, and amongst the April Fool's Day jokes, we are still together over forty three years, sorry to disappoint Joan and Derek, who gave us six months!!! 'Oh how i enjoyed, rubbing her long snooty nose in it, it was better than sex, as my husband said.

Although we had to wait for five years, before we could get married, I wanted to give Jim a baby of his own, and the word's he said, 'This is my second baby,' Barry is the first, he has been since he was born! We had found out when we had been together, for two years, that Joan had told Jims first wife about me, and that was why we had to wait for five years, not the two we expected to, because she wouldn't give him a divorce, although Jim was divorcing her on the grounds of adultery, having found her in bed with some-one else, she was furious when she had found out that me and Jim were getting married, but we waited, together for five years because then, if both party's don't agree to part, then we had to wait five years, because that was the law then, but our love for each other is still the same, if not stronger. Jim has two brothers, Tommy and John, who are brilliant, so are their wives, Edie, Tommy's wife and Corrine being John's wife, Them two being the youngest, who i might add, are now my only family beside's my own kids, and the love of my life, my Jim!! As at that time, i didn't know how much i was going to need them, Tommy, John and their wives, accepted Barry without question or judgement, and for that, i will till the day i die, always love them all.!! But as for Joan, to me she was dead, because i hated her even more in the years to follow, but at the time, i didn't know why, that was yet to come!

Jimmy was working in a place called BIBBYS, a soap factory when i first met him, and i went back to work, when Barry was nine months old. I was in my own place then, and getting social security payments, out of that, there was rent and everything to pay, so i decided to go back to work myself, mum said she would have Barry, 'there were no other kids at that time,'. I was working in a place called PLESSY'S, in WILSON ROAD, SPEKE, not too far away, which made components called Toggles, that went inside telephones, so when Jim said they were doing packing for the company, AVON, he would bring stuff up to me that were not passed, and i would sell it in work. This went on for a few months, until Jim got a job in FORDS, right behind the flats where i lived, then he got his brother John a job, but before John started, they went on strike for ten weeks, which didn't please Jim, because he was only getting five pound a week, old money, strike pay, which he had to give his mum, it meant he couldn't come and see me as much, so we decided that he move in with me, after all, it was a brand new two bedroom flat, which again didn't please Joan, because it meant she would have to pay her mother, more keep, and she was saving for her fantastic wedding. Oh i really felt sorry for her. NOT! IN NO WAY SHAPE OR FORM.

I had only started to dislike her when she took it out on my son, she just didn't want to know him, from the first time she saw him, she wanted nothing to do with him, and that really made me mad, after all, he didn't ask to be born, so fuck Joan TURRELL, now SERVICE . . . . When James came along, there were a few problems we had to deal with, concerning Barry, who was in the infants school at this time, because he was five now, and i only realised when James was two, that him and Barry, where both the same size, but at that time, it was a dinner-lady, with whom i was to become good friends, Edie Harris, she said to me one day at the school, 'He's not half cute,' she said everyone would laugh, in a nice way, but that didn't please me, to think he was being ridiculed at school. The following day, i took him to my GP, and took James along too, then i explained what had been said, and he measured their height and weight, there was only an ounce between their birth weight i told him, Barry was 7lb 15oz and James 7lb 14oz at birth, so he referred to ALDER HEY children's hospital, to see a professor White, and his registrar DR Colin Smith. That was the start of two years of tests, and my heart went out to Barry, because of the taunts he had to put up with, from cruel kids, and even worse, some of his teachers.

He was in and out of hospital, every other month, for test after test, and at one time when i went to see him, now on my third pregnancy, i walked into the ward, and at that very minute, i saw a nurses aid, or orderly as they were called then, she was just about to smack him, and i felt sick with temper, 'Don't you fuckin dare attempt to hit my son', you fuckin evil bitch, i said, and as soon as i got to the bed he was in, i noticed his hands were tired to each corner of the bed, i went berserk, as soon as i opened my mouth, everyone came running out of the office, telling me to calm down. "Calm down" why the bloody hell is he tied to the bed? 'While you fuckin lot are sitting on yer arses, he is left here bloody screaming,' And yer telling me to fuckin calm down! 'Get me a fuckin doctor,' NOW! I bent down to get his stuff out of the cupboard, when Dr Smith came to me, asking me why i was so upset, 'I just looked at him and snarled, pointing to the way i had left the bandages were they tied to, "You ask why im upset? Just look, or did you already know! "Anyway", im taking him home now, he's not staying here to be treated like a dog'. He just stood there, and he said he needed to explain about the results of tests they had done, so when Barry knew he was going home with me, he calmed down a bit, which was more than i had, but i listened to what he had to say. Dr Smith went on to tell me that x-ray's had shown that Barry's bone age was two years behind, so he told me that Barry had stopped growing when he was two, and they weren't sure if he would stay that size, or he might need some help with a hormone treatment, so i would have to take him back, at that time, every month, just to check his growth. I just sat there and i cried and cried, my poor Barry, not knowing there was worse to come, or was there?

PART TWO

∞

MY STAR SHINES ON

I couldn't take in, what the doctor had told me, or was it because i didn't want to believe it? I didn't know. He seemed happy enough, and he was made up when i gave birth to another boy, whom we called Paul John, after Jim's brother, and he was the double of his dad and the only one born with hair, pure black just like his dad, Stan, Jims dad said he was a typical TURRELL. Both Barry and James were born without a hair on their head, and when it did grow, they were both snow white blonde, they looked like twins, so i dressed them the same most of the time, not thinking they both had their own identity. When Paul was checked by the doctor, to see if he could go home, forty-eight hours after he was born, and because his weight was not as big as the other two, being only 6lb-13, he was a bit jaundiced, but ok to go, i couldn't wait to get home. That night we had all stayed at mums, and we were all in bed, when the baby, Paul, started screaming, and we tried everything, even feeding him, until it woke everyone in the house up. I would go downstairs with him, because i couldn't settle him, not even with a bottle until in the end, mum told me to get the doctor out. After only being home for a few hours home, we were on our way to the hospital, again, and it was the start of a very long stay, four months in fact, because it turned out that Paul could not get any nourishment from his food, it was going right through him, till they found he was allergic to any kind of milk, and so they tube fed him with soya, until he was old enough to take solids.

When the time had come to take Barry back to see his doctor, he then told me that they thought Barry would benefit from growth hormones, done by injections three times a week, but he would grow with this treatment, they had sorted visits to our GP, when the district nurse would come out which was to be started that week, his days were on a Monday, Wednesday, and Friday, and when he came home from school, he would have to wait in until the nurse had been, which he wasn't too happy about. Every time he got weighed, I would be the one to get told off, because he was putting too much weight on, and because he wasn't growing, he had to keep it down, but if he was staying at mothers, which was most of the time anyway, because she spoilt him, which i knew was out of guilt, having told me to 'Get rid of it', she would have put him in a glass case if it made her feel better, then she would give him anything he wanted, and didn't care less that i told her she would make him ill, and when he was staying there, he would drink up to four pints of fresh milk a day, and thats what put the weight on him, even though i had warned her that i wouldn't let him stay again, but it fell on deaf ears, as usual.

In the end, i had to stop Barry staying at mums on a school night, she wasn't too happy about it, but my son's health had to come first. James and Paul where a pair of little bleeders, it got so bad that, when they went to bed, we had to put a bolt on the outside of their bedroom, they would wait until everyone was asleep, because the door wasn't locked until then, we would get up in the morning, and every day without fail, everything, would be out of the cupboard and fridge, the likes of tea, sugar, butter, then soap-powder, and washing up stuff, it would all be on the floor, mixed together, thats why we had to use a bolt, the last resort.

Paul had to go one better, he was only two and a half, when he decided he liked buses, so much so, that every time he saw a bus pulling up outside our house, he would hop on it, and take the family pet dog, PAL, who really was Barry's dog, but while he was at senior school by then, the dog would follow Paul everywhere, and i would be out of my mind with worry for two or three hours, till i had to phone the police . . . It got that bad, i needed eyes at the back of my head with him, and the slightest chance he got, he'd be gone, till in the end, the bus drivers who did that rout, got used to him, that all the police had to do, was get through to that bus, and they used to laugh then drop him off outside our house, the little get thought it was funny.

Mum started to get up to her little tricks then, she would buy an outfit for just Barry, but never the other two, until Jim lost his temper one day and sent it back to her saying, 'We have three kids', not one,' and he was right, she never gave a shit about the others and never did! Like i said, she did it out of guilt and spite, because i never let her forget what she said. One day, i would be in the shopping arcade, in LEATHERS LANE, and i might have been caught without say a penny or two pence, then i would say, 'Mum, have you got so, so, because i never had enough or no change, then two months down the line, she would say, 'you owe me four quid', and i'd say, but i haven't borrowed any money,' then she would get this little book from her bag, and show me, every one or two pence that she had 'gave' me, was written down, and dated, then added up and she would tell me it was two or three pound, knowing i couldn't afford to pay her,. Fuckin hell, talk about spite, she was evil. I couldn't believe how mean she was, but when i look back at my earlier years, yes, she was always the same, but only with me. As Barry was under-going treatment, i felt relief, for him mainly, because he would get picked on because he was small, but one day i was doing washing, when he came running in during dinner-time crying, and when i asked him what was wrong, he just said that one of his teacher's had called him a little runt, and as i have said before, im a thick shit, because i didn't even know what a runt was, but Barry did, thats why he was upset. I ran up to the school and in slippers and apron, and demanded to see his art teacher, when the head-master asked why, i just said get him here now, or i'll go and find him myself, so he went to get him, while i waited, with smoke coming out of my ears, then the minute he walked in, i just pounced on him." What did you call my son? I roared at him, fuckin tell me, then the head-master told me to calm down, but i just ignored him, and when the teacher told me that he called Barry a little runt, i took one step back, then i swung round and i punched him with every five knuckles on my hand, when he said he would have me prosecuted, i said "Do what the fuckin hell you want, because my son takes enough shit from kids, and he doesn't need to hear your fuckin mouth doing the same, so then i told the head-master, not to expect Barry back, because he wouldn't be back. As soon as Barry was sixteen, he got himself a job.

Barry was working now, in a place called TULLY'S at the top of the lane, it was a garage and he loved cars. He loved the place, and fixing cars became a big part of his life. But later in life, his obsession was towards computers, he knew them inside out. But as i say, that was later on in his life. He had so many hurdles to get over first. Along the way, i had given birth to another son, Anthony, he has a middle name, but i wouldn't waste ink saying it, but that is part of another story! We were living in yet another maisonette, in a nice area, of Halewood, called PENMANN CRECENT, when Barry was just turned sixteen, i told him that i was pregnant, again, then his humour stepped in, "You two are disgusting, at your age". I was only bloody thirty four, but to Barry, we where old age pensioners. His wicked sense of humour was very dry, but he was so funny, that even on your darkest day, he would have you laughing, you just couldn't help but laugh at his antic's.

He would not let anyone get to him, with regards to his size, so it came as no surprise, when one day he came in and announced he was going to Newmarket, with a friend called Mick Irish, who lived a few doors away from us then. He wanted to train to be a Jockey, because he was small in stature, and that was more or less all he needed, except he would have to lose a bit of weight, because he was still chubby, but i didn't think he was over-weight, but his doctor at the hospital insisted that he carried on with the growth hormone treatment, plus they increased the dose, so he wasn't too happy about that. After a few weeks, just being accepted at Newmarket, the hospital sent me a letter, asking me why Barry hadn't attended his appointments, i was shocked, because they told Barry and my-self, that he was now old enough to attend on his own, but i found out that he wasn't going because my mother would hide him, if he didn't want to go, that was the beginning of another row, which ended up with me falling out with her then, because she was not worried what she was doing with his health.

When Jims brother, John and his wife were married, they gave us a video of the wedding, and when i look at it, i thought Barry and James looked very cute, both dressed in black velvet suits, which i had made for them, plus little black bow ties, they looked adorable, and yet i got upset again, because they were both the same exact size, and that was when i found out that Barry had stunted growth and his doctors blamed me for it, because i smoked while i was pregnant with him. In November, 1983, my baby was due on the 5th, when my waters had broke on their own, i got the fright of my life, because i thought something was wrong, as with the four boys, the hospital always had to start me off, and i didn't know what to do. I was already in the hospital, being admitted early hours of the morning, that day, and i was sitting in the smoke room, with other girls, some who had had their babies, some didn't, me being one of the latter, when one of the girls told me there was a puddle on the floor under me, i felt something warm on my legs, but never gave it any thought, so someone went and got a nurse, and by this time, i was getting scared, just in case i had done something wrong.

I was taken back to my bed, and the staff nurse said it was my waters, which meant the baby was on its way, or so i thought, so when this doctor came to see me, she told the nurse that i had wet the bed, then the nurse said, "I think you know the difference, between urine, and body water doctor" which she didn't like, she snapped at the nurse. "Well send her down to the labour ward then," and just walked away. That labour lasted four days, the pain was horrendous, but they wouldn't give me anything, at twelve thirty that Tuesday night, a lady doctor had me checked, and said, "Oh just leave her, she'll have a normal delivery, Then she went home. That was the 8th of November at ten o'clock that night.

The early hours of Wednesday, the 9th of November, as Jim was sat with me, after being told by phone that i had gone into heavy labour, i was exhausted, so was the baby, plus the baby was in distress, i was too tired to push, when in walked a big Greek bloke walked in, introducing himself to Jim, saying he was a surgeon, who proceeded to tell Jim, that my life and the baby's was at risk, and asked him to make a choice, if it came to that, did he want to save me, or the baby.! Poor Jim must have Shit himself, and i was too out of it to care, but what the surgeon said next made my hair stand on edge. "So, Mr TURRELL, we have to operate now, she needs emergency surgery, now. Jim said, "My wife". Next thing i knew, he said to Jim, 'This will be your fifth child", do you want her tubes done, while she's under? But i never expected the reaction, he got from Jim, all i saw was Jims head nodding yes." You Bastard! I called him, next thing, i saw these bleedin blue socks going on my feet, then Jim was asked to leave the room, while they got me ready, then he began to give me an internal, and i screamed, 'what are you doing,? I thought he was pulling the baby out there and then. He told me that he had to break my back water bag, the fluid that protected the baby, and there was i thinking he was gonna come out of my bloody mouth. I called my dearly beloved husband, every bastard under the sun, putting me through this. Then a nurse came in and she had two cards in her hands, one blue, one pink, saying, 'Have you got any names for your baby dear',? 'Oh yeh, as if i had time to sit and go through names, just put him down as Philip, it's another boy anyway'. Then i was taken to theatre, when they thought i was under sedation, they started to cut, that was till i screamed, then i heard them talking, then darkness.

At 3-45am Wednesday 9th November, my baby was safely delivered, and taken straight to the baby care unit, while i was still in theatre, being stopped from having anymore kids, knowing full well that i would have gone on trying, to have a daughter. The next thing I remember was Jim trying to wake me up, but i told him to fuck off, but he carried on. We've done it Mac, we've done it! 'We have got our little girl', 'Oh piss off.! It's another bloody boy,'! I was put in a room on my own, then when i did wake up, there was this little photo of my baby, so small, she looked like a doll, she only weighed just over a bag of sugar, and when i saw the name on the photo, i screamed, 'you can get that off for a start, the name Margaret. Jim was just sat there waiting, when the nurse came out with the baby, on her way to the baby care unit, when the nurse came back, Jim had forgotten to ask what sex the baby was, then she had to run back to the baby unit, but before she did, she said to Jim, 'Oh you're the man with four boy's! 'Jim went to go with her, but he wasn't allowed to follow her in, so she told him to wait by the door, then she came out of the room, and gave him a thumbs up sign, meant to tell him that he had a daughter,! I was to hear that Jim was walking towards the door, and headed toward the exit, when the nurse suddenly asked him. 'Are you not going to wait and see your wife, Mr TURRELL? 'Oh god forbid,' he had got what he wanted, stuff me. He came back in the afternoon with 125 congratulation's cards, and even one of him, which shocked me more, as with any of the boys, i never got one. Mother had been all over the estate, telling everyone that knew us, from then the cards started rolling in, even off mum, who told me i was a stupid bastard, wanting a girl anyway, 'their nothin but bleeding trouble'. Jim took me down to the baby care unit, as i hadn't seen my baby yet, I felt like a bleeding geriatric, having gone through two operations, so he had to take me in a wheel-chair, when we got there, we had to put gowns and gloves on, to save spread of infection.

The first time i held my daughter, i was petrified because she was so small, and she was wired up to all kinds of machines, the nurse told me she was six weeks premature, and that was all, so she took her out of the cot, and put her in my arms, i couldn't describe how i felt, but i fell in love with her then and there, and to this day, she is still my baby, even at the tender age of twenty seven on her next birthday. No man will ever be good enough for her, well that's my opinion anyway. After all visitors had gone, one of the girls that was in the smoke-room, when my waters had broke, came in my room, to see how i was, her baby boy being born three days earlier, i was still feeling weak, but i badly wanted a cig and i asked this girl, can't remember her name, anyway i asked her to help me into the bathroom, so i could have a smoke. The antic's out of us had us both in fits of laughing, was so funny, and because she was still sore, and i was like doubled over, i couldn't stop laughing and she just stood there and pissed herself, i was on the floor, after i had a couple of drags on the cig, that it made me sick to the point, where i blacked out, so a nurse had to get us both back into bed, but i hurt all over, but it was worth every stitch that stuck in me every time i moved. When i had been in for three days, i got the shock of my life, in walked Jims sister, the witch i hated, and dozy Derek, fuckin hell, i was gob-smacked. She put two little dresses on my bed, one from her, and one from Jims mum, then i said 'Bloody hell' it takes a daughter to fuckin get something,!

The lads got nothing, so i told her to take them back, Just as she was walking out of the ward, Jim came in, beaming from ear to ear, he said to her, 'Do you want me to take you to see my little girl? 'No she said, we've already seen her, then they left, and i told Jim what she brought with her, and what i told her to do with them, and that she was just passing, on her way to a party, so thats why she called in. 'How did she know where the baby was anyway i said, because they would have told me if she had phoned, so she hadn't been to see her, and was later confirmed later, when Jim took me to see her. From then on, i was allowed to feed her, but only in the baby unit, because she was still not taking enough milk, and she couldn't join me on the ward, which was disappointing, as all the other mothers had their babies with them, except me, but as i was up and walking, albeit very slowly, i was able to go and sit with her, and feed her when-ever i wanted, for as long as i wanted.

Her name caused a bit of a stir between me and Jim, he wanted her called Margaret, after me, not forgetting his mother, also called Mac, by his dad, but i was having none of it. 'She can have it as a second name', and that's it i said, her name is ANNE-MARGARET, since my sister had pinched the name i always wanted, if i had a girl, it was SUZANNE, who is now my niece.

I had been in hospital for over two weeks, and i had the baby with me, from two days before, when i demanded that i wanted to go home, but they told me i could go, but the baby had to stay for another couple of days, 'why i asked, she's ok now,? They told me she was a little jaundiced, so she needed this special lamp on her, but i was having none of it, i was going bleeding stir crazy, being stuck in there, so i told them on the Sunday morning, that we were going home, and they needn't try and stop me. I phoned home and told Jim to bring mine and the baby's going home clothes in that afternoon, and by six o'clock, we where home.

Barry was sat there like lord muck, but as i handed him his sister for the first time, he beamed at her, then said to me, 'Thanks for given me a sister, but don't ever put me through that again'. 'Put you through it' 'oh i do beg your pardon, sir! 'Have you been going for your injections? I asked him, he was due to pick another three month's supply from the hospital, and then go to the doctors every other day, The growth hormone had started to work, so when i found out that he hadn't been going, i flipped, and once again, it was mums fault,! That's it, i said, i'll take you my bloody self if you miss one more, then i started on mum. 'You're not fuckin helping him yer know, he needs to have them, and they are doing him good. Or would i live to regret saying them words!!!

KEEP SHINING MY STAR

In July 1984, we were given our first house, and i loved it, although we live in Runcorn now, i never wanted to leave that house, but mother was to blame once again, for because of her evil ways began to show itself again, but she had gone too far this time, and something i would never forgive her for, not as long as i have breath in my body!! When we had been in the house a few weeks, something happend to change the course of my life, Jim had been on the committee at the local labour club, we had been going there since we got together, and we always sat with who we thought were our friends, for over sixteen years. We done everything together for as long as i could remember, and all of them were part of the committee, in one way or another, we even went on holidays together, and every APRIL, when it always fell on our anniversary, we would all go for long weekends, or piss ups, as we called it, because we never took any kids, it was just adults, but we would take the kids in the September, when it was a bit more lively for them. It was always PONTINS in Southport, and we were worse than kids when we had been drinking, Anyway, being part of the club, Jim was compare or his full title was M.C. plus he was the bingo caller, and all their wives or girlfriends, would get free bingo tickets, and all the rest of their families would as well, although they were not supposed to, but it was kept quiet, although everybody did it, they all did. Jim was in charge of booking bands or singers, amongst other things, and he also knew who was fiddling the tax and everything else that was done under the table. One

Saturday, we never went out, but Jim had already made sure that mum, who was always with us, only because she never paid for a drink, and my sister Ann, anyway, this one night, the one we never went out, mum and Ann had already took their bingo cards out of mums bag, and after the game was over, they were asked where they had gotten their bingo cards from, so they told the chairman that Jim had got them, so then they were told to leave, which they did, and came straight to our house to tell us what had gone on. Jim wasn't bothered really, as we knew they all saw that all their families got them, but mother told us that they had been barred from the club, and not allowed to go again.

When we walked into the club the night after, we knew right away there was something going on, and before we even had time to take our coats off, he was called into the office, where all his so-called mates were sat down, the next thing, he came storming out, and he told me we were going, so when i asked why, he told me that he, not me, was barred for life, again with the lame excuse about the bingo tickets, which he admitted too, so he took the blame for mother and Ann, so they could go back in. I looked at the faces of our so-called friends, and not one of them could look me in the eye, or Jim, 'you fuckin shower of back-stabbing bastards', i said, call your-selves fuckin mates,! "Your nothing but shit, the lot of you", then i made for the office, where the bastards sat and told them and their chairman, who and when, they told me to get the bingo tickets for their families, it wasn't for that they wanted Jim out of the club, it was because he knew too much, so when they said to me that i could still go to the club, i got my membership card out of my bag, tore it up and threw it in their faces, telling them where to shove it. They wanted a Scape-goat, and they made it out on Jim. That was the last time we ever spoke to any of them.

After that night, mum was allowed back in, but felt uncomfortable, because everyone was looking at her, so she stopped going there. There was another club who were interested in Jim, because he was good at what he did, but because it was a catholic club, she didn't want to go. At last i thought, on our own for a change. But she wasn't that easy to get shut off.

We had been going to St Marks social club for a few months when in the October, the 25th, It was Barry's eighteenth birthday, and we gave him a little surprise birthday party, plus we had bought him his first car. It was not new, but we knew he would love it, it was a white Marina, which we hid out the back, so when he came in that way from work, he would see it, so we sat and waited, and waited, till we heard his key in the door. He came in, asking whose the car was parked up, then we wished him a happy birthday, and i threw him the keys to the car, he couldn't believe it was his, and the look on his face spoke a thousand words. Anyway, i said, 'Go and have your bath, then you can go for a run in it,' hurry up, then when he walked into his room, we heard all of his friends singing happy birthday to him, then i heard 'Aye mum, you could have warned me, I'll kill you. "Well it wouldn't have been a surprise then, would it, anyway, me and your dad are going out so have a good time. The beer is in the fridge.

Mother wasn't too happy, which was nothing new, but she had something up her sleeve, and we were not to find out for a couple of weeks. I loved the house we were living in, and even more so, when we had a fire place built, although it was only ornamental, the difference it made was amazing. As always, nothing good was to last in my life, my so-called mother always made sure of that, but what she did this time was beyond evil, if that were possible. Mother would be up every day, all day if she had her way, and all she did was moan and moan and moan, to the point when i would have to make an excuse to get rid of her, or cause an argument, in which case was the only thing that worked, and it would result in her walking out and nearly taking the doors with her. We had been in the house for six months, and the more we did to it, the more i loved it, then mother dropped her bomb-shell, and it scared the life out of me. One day she came up, and as normal, she would sit there in the kitchen, strumming her finger-nails on the table, which she knew went through me, and i asked her to stop, then out of the blue she said, "Don't you think it's about time you told Barry who his real father is"! I couldn't believe i was hearing this. "What the bloody hell do you mean? I said, Jims his dad, always has been, since he was a week old,' "No she said, his real father" and when i realised what she meant, i froze, "He doesn't need to know that, the bastard is dead anyway, which he was. Alan Smith, the piece of shit that raped me! He had died of a blood clot on the brain, about four months after i had Barry, and now she wanted him to know about it. Barry was known as my maiden name, but we had his name changed by deed poll, when me and Jim got together, only because Jim didn't want Barry to turn against him, but he had been known as a TURRELL, all his life, not just when we got his name changed, he went right through school with that name, so why was she doing this to me,? Why now, Barry was eighteen, what did she hope to gain from this, that fuckin evil bitch, how much can you hate someone, because i would have liked to have known then. I told her to get the fuck out of my house, and her parting words were, "If you don't tell him, I will"! And i thought a piece of shit was dead, but there was still an even bigger piece alive, and she called herself his grandmother, and worst of all, that shit, was my own mother. But i would make sure she would live to regret her words, so help me god, i would.

That night, me and Jim were in the kitchen, and between sobs, i was trying to do the kids tea, and i was dreading hearing Barry's key in the door. "We have to do this" i said to Jim, because that evil bastard is not goin to do it. She had already been up that day, and she brought her precious fuckin daughter Teresa, who was living in Runcorn at that time, but mother had got her to come and talk some "sense into me", as if i'd let her tell me what to do, what the fuckin hell do you think your goin gonna do".? "Don't you dare come in here," and I told you to fuckin stay away from here, now FUCK OFF NOW, and take her with you. I knew now why she was doing this now, it was because we had talked about moving to Runcorn in the past, before i got my house, and she didn't want Barry to come with us, she wanted him to stay with her, but she would soon have her answer. As Barry came through the front door, Jim called him into the kitchen, and we both told him, together, i told him what the sperm donor had done, as my daughter was to call him in later years, that i was raped, and that i was sorry for not telling him, but he was dead anyway. "Barry said he didn't care, as far as he was concerned, Jim had been his dad, and always would be, but he wanted us to promise him one thing, he didn't want the other kids to know, because he didn't want to be known as a step-brother, which we told him, there is no such word as STEP, he was their eldest brother, and always would be.!!! Oh my god, i couldn't wait to see her fuckin miserable gob, and rub her nose in the shit, where she belonged. It was thirteen years before she had even spoke to Teresa, because she had married someone that she didn't like. Then one day she wanted to find her and then i knew why she had asked me to go with her to find her, but not thinking, i went along with it. Although we knew she lived in Runcorn, and only a hint of where she lived, but when we did find her, it was to find that her husband was in prison, but for how long for, we didn't know, but she did get a shock when she opened her door, and saw mother and myself standing there, well you would wouldn't you, after thirteen years.? And since then, they became best friends, but it wasn't to last. She always fell out with one or the other, and make you suffer, and it always seemed to be me. But this time, she had gone too far with me, and i couldn't wait to tell her Barry's response, to what i had to tell him, and i knew then it would crush her, as i hoped it would, as she did to me. It then dawned on me, she had only done this out of spite, because we could still go out at the week-end, to St Marks, were Jim was now compare, doing everything that he did where we used to go, but she didn't like the place, so she wouldn't go out as often as she did, plus she would have to pay for her own drinks, where-as before-hand, Jim used to pay for her, so it was a coincidence that now she planned her evil deed. This so she thought, thinking Barry would turn against Jim, but she was in for a shock.

Before we had got our lovely house, it was after yet another row with mother, when we spoke about moving either back to Liverpool or Runcorn, because i had finished with my mother's butting in our lives, but Jim wouldn't budge, he wanted to stay in Halewood. The ultimatum she had given us over Barry, was the last straw because Jim said to me 'Do you still want to go to Runcorn', it broke my heart to leave that house, but i said yes, because i wanted to get as far away from her as i could, but i had one last thing to do.!! I asked Barry did he want to come to Runcorn with us, and he said 'Where you go, i go'. Then i had everything i could have asked for, so armed with all my good news, i marched down to mothers, and told what Barry had said about his sperm donor, and our decision to move, away from her, and she could take the fuckin smirk of her face, because Barry wanted to come with us, and not stay with her, but the best bit was watching the colour drain from her face.

So twelve months to the day, 7th July 1985, we moved to Runcorn. We only waited four months for a four bedroom house, because if you had family already living there, then you would get a place quite quick. Me and Teresa were back on speaking terms, so it was her husband Casso, as we knew him, but his first name being John, was the man who had hired a van, and when the day came, he was there, and as soon as everything was loaded, we were gone. It felt weird crossing the Runcorn bridge, i felt as though i was emigrating, going on the opposite side of the Mersey, yet so sad, that i had been forced into leaving my lovely house, but excited at the same time, but i never knew that soon, i would wished i had stayed where i was.

DIMMING LIGHT

As Barry had turned eighteen, he was now an adult, which meant he could no longer attend Alder Hey for his injections, so he was transferred to The Royal Liverpool Hospital, under a Mr Johnson. It was during this year, in fact only a couple of months, when the kids were out, and Anne was in bed, that we watched a program about growth hormone, and what the government tried to cover up about the drug. It was leaked out, that one person in a million contracted a terminal disease, called C.J.D. then not knowing the full name of it, at the time, i called Barry from his room, where he was doing work on his computer, 'Have you seen this'? He stood and listened for a few minutes, then he said 'Don't want to know', and went back into his room. We found out the name for this disease, which was called Creutzfeldt-Jakob-Disease. As we sat and watched the program, we thought, oh it's only one in a million, that shouldn't harm Barry. We had been told when Barry first started the treatment, that it was expensive, but it would be beneficial to him in terms of his growth, so his treatment carried on, and even his dose was increased. And Barry carried on receiving the treatment until 1985, and as he got older, he had the growth hormone at home, and was injecting himself, so no-one thought any more about it, and it was put to bed, for a while anyway. Also, there was no reason to think, or any evidence that there was anything wrong, so we just carried on with our lives. He had grown, so it was working, and i could never had been happier, at last, my son could have a normal life. That was all that mattered as far as i was concerned. I had got myself a job in a small factory, called SKEMBACK, on the ASTMOORE estate, only cleaning at first, but later on i was to be trained as a supervisor in the factory, in which we made the plastic containers for cosmetics, shampoo, and other things. It was August bank holiday, 1987, and i was at home, just doing the cleaning and washing, because that was the only time i would have, as i had started shift work, which i hated, but it had to be done.

I was kneeling down, when i felt my knee crack, and i cried out that i couldn't move, and then Jim came from the living room, and that was that, i couldn't carry on so i sat on the chair, with Jack, my daughters pet rabbit. He was almost human that rabbit, he didn't need a hutch, which he did have in the back garden, he would just come in and sprawl out in front of the fire like a cat would. We also had JESS, a GERMAN SHEPHERD, which had moved from Halewood with us, as Barry had bought her for forty pound at the time, and he idolised her. Anything he wanted her to do, he would train her till she got it right. He had taken his driving test, but the first time he failed, as he prepared for his second time, this time he passed and was over the moon. As i got ready for work after the bank holiday, my knee was so badly swollen, it was stopping me from doing my job, so when my boss came over to see what was wrong, i showed her the swelling, and she sent me home, from there i had to go the hospital, with Jim at my side, after an x-ray, we were told that i had Rheumatoid arthritis, and it had spread to other joints, so i could not work again, which was a blow, because Barry's 21st birthday coming up, but all was not lost, as i had gotten a loan from Provident, but said nothing, so then i was also told that i was entitled to something called Mobility, because i was now classed as disabled, and with it, also came back-pay of nearly five hundred pound, plus i would get the same amount every month.

After we had lived in Runcorn for exactly six weeks, my sister Ann moved up there, having got an exchange with two people we knew from Halewood, who wanted to move back there, so that meant mother would know where i lived, but it never bothered me now, because when we were forced to tell Barry that news, he knew then, what kind of woman his so-called grandmother was and i had made sure she knew. She was always a bitch, but only with me, but i didn't give a shit anymore, as long as she left me and my kids alone.

As far as i can remember, in fact i remember everything that woman did to me. As far as she was concerned, there was only two of her daughters had kids, not me or Teresa, it was Ann and Carol. At the time, Teresa was still living in Runcorn, and Carol who lived in WHISTON, with her then husband Barry Malone, although he was in prison, but i didn't know what for. So that left just me and Ann in Halewood. Ann had two kids, Warren and Suzanne, she was the one who bore my choice of name for my daughter, then, there were Carol's three kids, again there was Barry, called after his dad, then Carla, and Sarah. These were the only grand-kids my mother had, She proved this one night, when at one time, we never had a penny, and i would rather have sold something from my house, than ask her to lend me money, and when this one time i did ask her, it was when Barry had gone to visit her, so he had his tea while he was there, but the others hadn't had anything, it was what she did next, that broke the camel's back, she had me in tears, because she knew from Barry, that i had nothing to eat for my kids, and i had to beg her, and beg her, over and over, to lend me some money to buy some food for my kids, and it was when everywhere was closed, and it was too late to get anything, being nearly ten o'clock at night, she decided to lend me a fiver. It gave her a chance to have the last laugh on me, after i had told her to stay away from me, but my kids came before my pride, so i had to swallow it.

That had happend before we moved to Runcorn, so when i heard that Ann was moving to Runcorn, i went sick, not because of Ann, but knowing that my mother would never be away from her, and i was right.

Even though she had not been to visit Teresa before, Carol was the next one to move from WHISTON, and it was only then she said she had no choice now that we all lived away from her, so she would come up once on a Wednesday, but only to see Barry, before Carol had moved, she would go and see her on a Tuesday and Sunday, but when Ann moved, it was right at the back of me, so when she came to see her, she would stay all fuckin week, and she would never leave us alone. As we had been more or less settled, by the time Ann moved up, baby Anne was hypo, so we used to give her a spoonful of medicine, just to calm her down so she would fall asleep, then i would carry her up to bed. After a while, i started to speak to my mother, but i warned her before-hand, if she ever did or said anything to me or the kids, then she would be out the door again.

JUNE 1996

Barry had received a letter from Dr Colin Smith, from ALDER HEY hospital, to tell him that his growth hormone, was almost certainly contaminated, and if he wanted to, he could go and see him, or he could seek advice from a councillor, concerning the likelihood of the out-come of his treatment, which at that time, he had been on for ten years, the letter Barry had got, he kept hidden, he had received it in FEBUARY 1992, and i was only to find out about it in the months ahead. He and my sister Carol had grown up together, and were more like brother and sister, so it didn't surprise me that he had confided in her. I knew he had been going for hospital's for different tests, but he had been doing that for years, so i never thought nothing of it, but the only thing that did bother me, was that he never bothered with girls, i used to joke with him, 'Aye Barry, are you gay, id ask? All he had ever wanted, was to have children of his own, but even that was snatched away from him, because he had already been told that he would never be able to father a child. For his birthday, the previous October, we had bought him a beautiful jet black German shepherd bitch, whom he called Jazz, and he idolised her, she went everywhere with him, and he taught her everything that he had with Jess, till she passed away, in January 1995. He was to go in for more tests, this time in WALTON, to have brain scans, and it was that day that i got the news that would take the very heart out of me. It shook me to the core. My sister came into my bedroom, and she just broke down, and she told me what i already knew in my heart. It is crucifying me writing this, but i have to.

Carol had told me, that he was praying that they would find something wrong with him, because with this horrible disease, it couldn't be detected until the brain itself was dead, and had an incubation period of up to thirty years, if not more. He had told Carol, that he was almost certain he had C.J.D. I just couldn't take it in.!!!!!

That day i found out that my Barry, my first-born and my world, was that one in a million. There never was and never will be again. The Most Bravest person, to walk this earth!! That was when my star went out!

7ᵀᴴ December 1996 — 2-15pm

LIFE WITH CREUTZFELD-JAKOB DISEASE

PART ONE

∞

MURDER

This part of my life, or more of an existence, is my memory of my son Barry.

The beginning of January 1996, Barry was admitted to Warrington hospital, for traction on his back, and as i knew what it was because i myself having had done on my back, and i had suffered with my back for years. I had found that the traction had done me the world of good at the time, so i thought it might be hereditary, anyway, i came home from work to find Barry on the floor, and he was in a lot of pain, so i had to get his doctor to come out, because he couldn't budge an inch, without pain, so when his doctor came, he told Barry that he would have to go in, so they could do other tests at the same time, but not for his back. He was in for a week, and he couldn't wait to get back to his beloved computer, he was obsessed with it, but that was what he had wanted to do. Barry had taken a computer course, for which he had taken a bank loan, and he worked on it every spare minute he could. He finished his course, and had gained city and guilds, plus other certificates until he couldn't go any higher, so the people who had taught him actually gave him his first job, in that field. It was a place called COMUTEACH. As he had taken his test, and passed at the second attempt, we bought him a second hand escort, then he went to be fitted for his first suit, i was so proud of him, so i went in search for a brief-case, which he would need for his job. On the day he started, i didn't know who was more excited, me or him. As he had just gotten changed, he put on his first ever tie and new shoes and shirt, he made his way toward the front door, so i followed him, just to see him off, he said to me, 'Mum, im not going to school, so there's no need to see me off you know', 'ok i said', and you could see his pride light up his face.

My two middle boys were away in the army, and then when the first gulf war came, off they went. I was never any good at sleeping then, i would just sit and watch Sky News constantly, I was just focused on the war. After i had left my job, i was riddled with arthritis, all over my body, and every joint was so painful that Barry would have to change bedrooms, his being on the ground because i couldn't climb the stairs. A doctor from another area came to see me at home, because at that time, i couldn't walk and all my fingers were all bent and twisted, also, i had to go into the hospital to have my knees drained, which i was petrified because they had to draw the fluid out of the bone, and i had bitten through the handle of my hand-bag, god that bloody hurt. I was told that the arthritis would spread, which it did, and would only get worse, not better. So that was my work up the spout, but i was told i would get an allowance every month called Mobility, which would get me a new car every three years, and it wouldn't cost me anything, because it was all covered, all i had to do was find myself a driver.

When all of a sudden Barry's ears stood to attention, he had his heart set on me getting a car, when i told him because i couldn't work anymore but i would get nearly four hundred pound a month, he said it would only cost just over one hundred pound a month for the car, and that he would give me the same amount back from his wages, i couldn't say no, so he went and picked the one he wanted, and then all we had to do now, was wait. The day arrived when me and Barry went to pick up the car, Barry couldn't contain himself, the look on his face told its own story, and as we drove home, all he said and kept saying, was "Brill", that was it. We exchanged from the big house we were in, to a bungalow, just down the other end of where we lived, and it was only because of my health, mainly my knees, because of the stairs, although i was giving up a four bedroom, and the bungalow was only three, it didn't really matter, with James and Paul being in the army, thats all that we would need, but Barry wasn't too happy to be moving at all. The night before we moved,

Jims brother John turned up, with his wife Corrine, to tell Jim that his mum had died, it seemed she fell and smacked her head on the floor, and it was their sister Joan who found her the next morning, having to get the police to break in. Jim never reacted the way i expected, he just got a bottle of whiskey and two glasses, handing one to John. We both went down after we had moved, and there wasn't anything we could do anyway, and i didn't want to be in his sisters company any longer than i had to be.

Barry was getting more and more involved with different hospitals, and was always on the internet, and if i asked why, he just said, 'Mind your own', and that was that. It was about six weeks after Jims mum died, that he was to find out his mum had left them each some money, but they had to wait until after probate, so he wouldn't know when he would get it. Barry was only in the bungalow four months, when he shouted me one morning, so i went into his bedroom, where he told me that the council had offered him a flat, and i was gobsmacked, because he had never even said he had applied for one, but he was in his twenties now anyway, it was his choice, and he wanted his independence, so who was i to argue. In February 1996, Barry was once more told go home, and stop wasting their time, 'there' nothing wrong with you'. Both of us were fuming. The flat Barry was offered, was in a place called Castle-Fields, just up the road, so i went with him to view it, and i think he fell in love with it, because within three days, he had moved in, and as he found out, he knew his friend from work, lived next door. We helped him all we could, with furniture and curtains and what-ever, and we also bought him a second-hand cooker and fridge, and anything else he needed, he got himself.

This was where Jazz grew up, and i was relieved that he had her, because it doesn't matter how old you are, no-one likes to live alone, but it felt weird, not having him around, or hearing his music, i told myself to grow up, because he had. His music he loved, and he had his favourite ones, mainly UB40, and a group i had never heard of, THE LIGHT-HOUSE FAMILY, the next was Simply Red. He lived in that flat for nearly four years, and that's when things started to happen, he would normally come down every day, with the dog, because she went every-where with him. I didn't want him to think i was watching his every move, so i was surprised when after a week he started to phone me, to take meals up to him from our chip-shop, because he didn't want to go out. I thought he was taking the piss, because i would have to go for his meal, then take the bus to his flat. One night, i had taken his meal up, which by now had become a habit. I asked him why he couldn't come down, because he had the car, and i had to get the bus, and my arthritis was getting worse. I was shocked to hear that he was scared to go out, 'Why, whats up'? He told me that his balance was getting worse, and that people would look or stare at him, assuming he was pissed, so he stopped going out, from that, everything got worse on a daily basis,.

From then on, i would do his shopping, and write his cheque's to pay his bills. July was the last time he had to go for tests, and got the same answer, all negative, so i think he more or less knew what that meant, he just convinced himself that he had this thing, this disease called C.J.D. But he made sure i was never told, he had confided in my sister Carol. From then, i started to ring around to find out all about this thing, but i wasn't ready for what came next. When my sister told me what Barry had told her, she had to tell me, i went cold, then screamed, and cried, when next Carol said to me, 'We'll have to tell mum', shall i call her in, i just nodded and she called her into my bedroom, Carol told her what she had told me, and what she said made me jump, all i heard her say was, 'Why Barry,? Why not one of the others? I couldn't believe my ears. 'It's bad enough that Barry had this horrible thing, but to wish it on one of my other kids, what an evil Twat she was. That night, taking Barry's meal up to him, with every intension of asking him why he felt he couldn't confide in me, my mind was somewhere else, and when i knocked on his door, i couldn't get any answer, and i started to worry, knowing that he wouldn't go out, i shouted through the letter-box, till i heard a shuffle, then the door opened, after what seemed forever. I stood behind him as he led the way to his living room i said to him, 'Why are you walking like that? He fed me some cock-bull story, and then i said its probley an ear infection. That was the last time he went out. All of a sudden, this girl came on the scene, whose name was Jackie, and was the sister of Peter, Barry's next door neighbour, and workmate. She told Barry that she had been living with her parents for two years, and was getting divorced. They became friends then, but later on, she told me that she had left her husband for Barry, which was a load of bullshit. I had been in touch with his housing officer and told them what was wrong and i was scared he might fall, and could they find him a ground floor flat, while in the meantime, this girl was moving into her brothers next door. She would go in at night, and according to her, they would talk all night, then she was getting ready to go to AMERICA with her mum and dad during the next few weeks, but she had forgotten a certain statement in no uncertain words that she had told me, when Barry was on his trip to Walton, and he asked me to ask her to look after Jazz for that week, the answer was 'Im sick of putting my life on hold for "him'.

I told her not to bother, i would take Jazz myself then i told her to go, otherwise i would have butted her. Then Barry would start on me, 'What did you say that for'? He said to me, after hearing the front door slam. 'Who the fuck does she think she is? 'She was so full of shit, and she was to prove it as Barry got worse. Ok, so they sat and talked, but to be a good liar, you have to have a good memory, which she seemed to forget. She knew i didn't like her she didn't like me, so what! I didn't give a shit, but there was no fuckin way i would let her take my son for a fool. She fooled everyone into thinking she loved Barry, including him, so i just went along with it because i didn't want Barry upset. While she was away, the housing office came up with a two bedroom ground floor flat, so we took him to see it. Any other time Barry would have loved it, but it was like he had given up, and that wasn't like him, all his fight had gone, he had just been carried away with it all. He had been getting some stuff out of a catalogue, like a fridge freezer, a new washing machine, and a three piece suite, which i know for a fact wasn't for him, because i had gave him the money to buy the wooden one he had, it was bought from a ware-house in Widnes. Barry was besotted, and couldn't see what she was up to, and nothing i said would make him change his mind. I went to see his best mate, ZIGGY who would know about things, because Barry would phone him, all hours asking advice on what to do about girls, he would ask how would he ask her certain things, or anything to do with girls, because he never had the self confidence to do it himself, because he had never had a girlfriend before. On the 23 September 1996, Barry moved into his new flat, or he went through the motions. We had stripped all the walls and decorated before he moved, even had the living room carpet and his bedroom done, so all he had to do, was wait with ZIGGY, then when it was all sorted, i phoned him and told him it was ready and waiting, all he had done was have a cup of tea, then he went to bed, and that was the last time he saw on the outside of his bed.

One thing ZIGGY told Barry, when he came to visit him, was to be aware of her, but i wasn't to find out about this till December. Barry had been in his new flat for nearly four weeks. I would go down as soon as i woke up, then i would stay all day because he couldn't be left on his own at that stage.

I had been ringing around to find out anything that would help Barry, i even wrote to his doctor at the WALTON CENTRE, a Mr ENERVOLDSON, but all i got was more lies, they were looking at tests that Barry had undergone, but found nothing, so he said, but i didn't believe him. One time i did manage to get to WALTON when Barry was in there, i found that Barry had been put in a room on his own, so i asked why, and was told that he had the MRSA bug, and they had other patients to worry about. Barry had wanted to go for a smoke, so we had to walk through a full ward to get outside, so what was all this about him having a bug, he was not allowed to leave his room, but he could if he had someone to take him, yet he was allowed to walk through a ward, so for Barry to have a bug, was a load of bullshit, they just put him in there in case someone caught anything from him.

I went back with Carol the day he came home from there, and he drove his own car, the first time in a long time, and i was over the moon. I was convinced he was getting better.

One day on my daily visits to Barry's, it was the day i was going to pay his bills and get his shopping, he told me that Jackie was cooking a meal for four, who consisted of himself, Jackie, ZIGGY and his wife and he was chuffed. I myself had my own opinion, but i didn't want to burst his bubble, because he seemed so happy. He told me to get a load of stuff that would be needed, including sirloin steak, and four large trifles, for afters, and i was happy to do it, because he was really excited and looking forward to it. This was her first visit to Barry's new flat since she had been back off her holiday, and it was three weeks after her return, so i wondered why she hadn't been over before, because if she loved him, and she knew he was ill, i would have thought she would have been sooner, but i said nothing. Barry's brother Tony, who stayed with him twenty four hours a day, and he would see to Barry's personal things like take him the toilet, and see to whatever a man needed, things i couldn't do. Barry asked the both of us not to be there, the night Jackie was doing the meal, so we just stayed there till five o'clock, and she would be there just about six. I was a bit worried leaving him on his own, because he was helpless on his own by now, and bedridden, but he said he could manage the phone if he needed me, and the phone was always on the bed anyway, so i let him have his own way.

During that night, i had rang the CJD helpline, there were things i needed to know, and the lady i spoke to was called DOT, who told me that her son had been a victim of the same debilitating disease, and had died only a few months before, but he had caught it through the meat chain, although the symptom's were the same. She passed my phone number to a councillor at GREAT ORMAND STREET hospital, who rang me later that night, and my fears were confirmed, her name was LIEHA DAVIDSON, and she started to tell me what to look out for.

That night, at the beginning of November, as LIEHA reeled off the sign's to look out for, was a night i will never forget, he will be unsteady on his feet, his vision would become blurred, his hand-writing would be next to go, he will have hallucination's to which i replied 'He's already had this and that, but as the list was getting longer, the worst was yet to come, and i was petrified that i was going to lose my son. I was saying to myself, it's only a dream, i'll wake up soon, but it wasn't a dream, it became very real. The following day, i went down to Barry's, and as i let myself in shouting, 'It's only me, just in case Jackie was there, and as i walked in the door, my eyes went straight ahead to the kitchen, where there was a lot of shouting and shuffling, and when i opened the door, i was horrified at what i saw.! Barry was stood by the table, and in his hand he had a walking stick, which he was using to hit Jazz, he just kept hitting and hitting her, at the same time, he was crying his heart out. It was so gut-wrenching for me to see, and i broke down myself, i had to shout at him to stop, then he just fell into a heap on the floor. As i helped him back into bed, i wondered how he had got to the kitchen in the first place, because there was no-one else there. I made him a cup of coffee, and got him settled, then i asked him why he was hitting Jazz, because he adored that dog, he told me that he was trying to turn her against him, and i said to Barry, he could never do that, because she too loved him, and later as she lay next to him on the bed, he tried to say to me, 'look at the loyalty from her', he cried. His muscle's kept going into spasm making his legs jump and caused him an awful lot of pain. I went to get him some pain-killers, and when i opened the fridge, i noticed that the stuff he had asked me to get the day before, for Jackie to cook the meal, was still there. I went back to Barry and asked him why it was still there, he just said, 'She never turned up! 'That fuckin bitch', just fucking wait till i get my fuckin hands on her, i was fuckin fuming. That poor lad, i sat in the kitchen and sobbed, i just couldn't stop. Just as i got Jazz ready to take her out for her walk, Tony came in, and within minutes, he had Barry laughing his head off, and when i heard this, i thought he's getting worse. From the time he found out about this illness, he went around everyone in Halewood, just to see them, and say his own little goodbye's, because he knew there was no cure, but not one of my so-called family, only Carol and her husband, and mother, once a week, had the fuckin guts or balls to come and see him, but then, knowing that lot, i never expected anything else. Another of Barry's friends started coming to see him when he could, as he was a nurse at our local hospital, and in the following weeks to come, i never realised how much we would need him. His name was Steven Williams, and he would sometimes stay over, when he wasn't at work, which gave Tony and my other son Paul who would take over from Tony as Barry got worse. When the other bitch Jackie finally showed her face, Barry asked me not to say anything, so i had to bite my lip every time she turned up, to the point where i had to walk out. Barry was getting worse day by day, there was always something different every day. The first week in November, out of the blue, i received a phone call from a solicitor called David Body, from Irwin Michelle's Solicitors in Sheffield, who had received a call from LEHA Davidson, the councillor who had been keeping in touch with me. He told me that he was in the process of taking legal action, against the DEPARTMENT OF HEALTH. He asked if he could make arrangements to come and see me and Barry, to which i agreed, after all, they would be responsible for the death of my son.

We had arranged for him and his secretary to come on the eleventh of November, to which Barry agreed. We were woken up early hours one morning, to find Jackie at the front door, Jim came in the bedroom and said that Barry was asking for me, so i was out that bed like a flash, when Jim said 'What do you want me to do about work? Fuck bleedin work i said, my son is more important, so off we went. 'Please god, not yet, let me have him a bit longer, i was very scared by this time, and my heart was breaking. I had never in my wildest dreams thought that i would be feeding my son at the age of twenty nine years of age, things were getting worse and i was so scared. We had to be there all the time now, we just couldn't take that chance. The day arrived when the solicitor was coming to my house, then from there i would take him down to Barry's flat. While i had the chance, i told the solicitor everything about this bloody Jackie, because there was no way i would let her take Barry for a ride, not while i had breath in my body.

When we got to Barry's flat, i made them a drink and because Barry couldn't hold a cup, he had to use a baby beaker. One thing Barry never done, was swear, never in his life did he swear in front of me, but i did hear from his friends, that he swore like a trooper, but he never even said bloody in front of me. He had too much respect for me, that, i did know. I was about to sit down when David Body asked if they could have some time with Barry on his own, i said that was fine and went into the living room. Because Barry could hardly speak now, it was a struggle to get his words out, so he had to shout, so i heard every word that was said anyway. I heard them telling Barry, that they were dealing with other people who had contracted CJD, and not all batches of growth hormone had been contaminated, but Barry's most certainly was. Then all i heard was, 'But she's already married to some-one else', meaning Jackie, then things went to a sort of whisper for a few minutes, then they both came out. David, as he told me to call him, told me that Barry had started to take action against the Dept of Health, the government in other words, and he had also made a will which they could not discuss of course, but i was shocked when i heard that he had wanted Jackie to be his executor to his will, plus Jackie was to have "EVERYTHING FROM A FORK TO A CARPET"!!! I fucking knew it, i knew it. She had Barry wrapped round her fuckin finger the bastard. I had to walk out because i was fuming, she's getting sod all. As i was going out the front door, she was just about to put a key in the door and i asked her how long she had a key, she said to me, 'Sorry, i thought you would have been gone by now! 'I fucking bet you did, you bitch'"! I went home for a bit so i could calm down, otherwise i would have done her some serious harm, but i went back after an hour. There was no way she was going to be left on her own anymore, not with Barry. When i got there, Steve was there, she wasn't, and Barry seemed upset, which was the last thing i wanted, then when i got to his bedroom, the phone rang in the living room, so i answered it and it was LEHA, the councillor. She rang to ask about Barry, then she went on to tell me about David Body. He was only doing his job, because all he cared about was getting compensation for the victim's and their families, she then went on about the stages that Barry would go through, and at that moment i screamed down the phone, 'I don't want their fuckin money, i want my son to live, at this point, everywhere had gone quiet, and i saw my son Paul, just standing there crying, Barry didn't know who he was, and this was heart-breaking. I was talking to LEHA, she was telling me about things that would happen, and then there was a click on the phone and i asked LEHA was it her, then Barry spoke 'It's me he said.' He asked if CJD could be caught through sex, and i was gobsmacked, i was listening to something private, but Barry told me to stay on the phone while he spoke to her, and the things he asked about, i felt so embarrassed, till he asked a certain question, then i knew why she was not there, Jackie had been told that she could have caught the disease by a certain sex act, so she had ran out and left Barry on his own, Steve had only just got there when i did. Barry asked LEHA if she could come and see him and Jackie, to put her mind at rest, because she had been told by somebody, that it was contagious so she just told Barry she would not be back, but when he told her that it wasn't true, and that LEHA was coming the following day, she made arrangements at work to be at Barry's around three pm.

For the last weeks of my son's life, he would not let himself fall asleep, just in case he didn't come back, meanwhile i phoned my second son James, and told him if he wanted to see Barry alive, then he should come to Runcorn right away, but because he was in NORTHAMPTON at that time, he could not get there, so he came on the first train the following morning. He arrived at my house because he hadn't been to Barry's new flat. He asked if he could go for a drink first because he was so scared, but i told him not to, because Barry didn't like the smell of drink, although he had the odd glass of wine now and again. It was this time that Barry told James, that he had seen his father, James asked him what he was talking about, he said my dad's at work, then Barry said to him 'Not your dad! Mine!!!!

I couldn't believe it, Barry had brought this up, and now it meant that i would have to break my promise that i had made to him, when he was eighteen. Now i resented my mother with a vengeance, but i said nothing, and the only one who knew about the situation for now, was James and he promised he wouldn't say anything till i was ready to tell the rest of my kids, then it was put on hold, because right then, Barry was more important. James went back home the next day, just to explain to his wife, STEPH, and my eldest grand-daughter NIKKI, so i asked him and his wife could he take ANNE, my daughter back with him, while i looked after Barry. But because it was Anne's thirteenth birthday the 9th November, i took her down to see Barry before she went. She knew he wasn't well, but that was all, and she was made up when she got a birthday card and twenty pound of him. Then because all her stuff was already sorted, off she went. James said he would be back in a couple of days. From that day, someone had to sit and be by Barry's side, and most of the time, it would be me or Tony, his brother. He kept his music on twenty four hours a day, so he wouldn't fall asleep, and if he felt himself slipping in and out, he would jerk himself back. This went on for four weeks. Barry was in a lot of pain, because he couldn't pass water, or use the toilet and this had gone on for nearly a week, because his stupid doctor told him that he would have to go the hospital, because he needed a catheter fitted to relieve his bladder. He was so distressed that i phoned the hospital, and they sent an ambulance, but he was adamant that he wasn't going to hospital, in case we left him there, even though i promised him we would bring him straight back home, he was having none of it. The paramedic's that came were brilliant with him, but they did explain that they would have to stay until the on call doctor came. When the doctor did arrive, it was one that i had met one time before, we just called her Sue, when we explained what was going on, she said she wouldn't be long, she just had to nip back to her car, and she came back with a catheter, and she had Barry a lot more comfortable in five minutes!

Then she came to me and asked me if i needed anything, and when i said no, she gave me a direct number and told me to ring her, for anything. The only thing i wanted, i couldn't have. A week after that, Barry was getting weaker by the day, he had refused any treatment what so ever, if it meant prolonging this horrible thing that was killing him, because he knew there was no cure, and he didn't want to linger. At one point, his friend Ste told me that Barry was getting eighty four painkillers a day from his doctor, until i went to see him, and as soon as i told him that Barry was going to try and commit suicide, it stopped, then when i asked Barry about it, he said to me 'that's a coward's way out',. Then i went through every drawer and collected all the tablets he had and i flushed them down the toilet. All he lived on, was chocolates, he even had his own 'Munch box as he called it.

Sometimes he would just lay there, after the nurses had washed him, but he would not let go of my hand, he nearly broke it, because he gripped it so hard. By now he was choking on his own saliva, and we had to suction it out, because he couldn't swallow, he was getting more tired, but would not loosen his grip on life, he clung on to every minute. It was like i was in the middle of a horror movie, this is something that happens to someone else, not to me, and certainly not to my son, he never deserved this, he had never brought me an ounce of bother. I thought i would wake up and it was all a dream, but we were not that lucky, it was reality. I lay on the bed sometimes, and he would lay his head on my shoulder, he just looked out of the window, or i would be sitting in the armchair by his bed, when he gripped my hand. I fell asleep once, with my head on the bed, when the bed shook, i shit myself, thinking every minute was the last, but he always jerked himself back, or his limbs would just take over, because he had no control over anything now. It was the third week in November, a Wednesday, the day his beloved nana came to see him. She knew which way to go now, so i would be at Barry's anyway when she arrived. I made her and Barry a drink, but he couldn't swallow it, so i just kept his mouth moist, and he was Meticulous about his nails and teeth, he asked me to clean them, which i did, and she never said a bloody word for over an hour, all she did was strum her nails on the end of the chair. 'When all of a sudden i heard, 'Nana, will you fuck off', I was so made up that i burst out laughing, and when Barry struggled to ask me what i was laughing at, i told him what he had said, he started to chuckle, and that made my day.

The 22nd of November, Barry's doctor from Walton Hospital came to see Barry and myself. He also asked that all the family be there. Mr ENERVOLDSON was there spot on four o'clock, along with Barry's own doctor, Dr OTIV, who just stood back against the wall and he looked as though he was standing to attention, but he couldn't look me in the eye, so i said to him 'What's up? Is your boss here, you're not the big man you think you are now, are you'. He never said a word. Both of them went in to see Barry, and the conversation went on for ten minutes then i heard Barry say 'Don't upset my mum'! I felt like i was choking, but as they came in and sat down, my legs just went from under me then the next thing i remember someone was wiping my face with a wet cloth.

This doctor who had told me by letter only two weeks before, that they didn't know what was wrong with my son, was now telling me that my son most certainly had CJD. 'You fuckin hypocrite, get out of this room, Now! 'You fuckin knew all the time what was wrong with him,' yet you fob me off with shit! Then i ran into Barry, and i cried and cried,

'Im so sorry BAZ, i cried, 'Why? It's not your fault! But i started you on them, but instead of helping you as i thought, i was killing you, and there's nothing i can do.! He just stroked my face and told me it wasn't my fault. I heard my son' Paul ask if Barry would see Christmas, and he said probably, but he would not be aware of it, and it would get a lot more harrowing! My sister Carol asked me to bring Christmas forward, so Barry could have it one last time. I was horrified, because to me, that would seem like celebrating he was dying and i told her no way.

Within the space of three days, Barry lost his sight, all movement of his body and his whole personality just changed completely. That wasn't my son! Whatever was on that bed, it wasn't my son. It was like something out of the EXCORTIST. I was scared out of my wits. You could actually see the life draining out of him. It was Friday 6th December, when i phoned his doctor and told him that he needed to come and see Barry, he was in a lot of discomfort now. He needed stronger pain relief. In six weeks, i had lost two stone in weight, but Barry kept his chubbiness, mainly because he had been bedridden for so long. The doctor came about half an hour after i had called. He went to check Barry, but there was something coming that would stay in me for the rest of my life. As the doctor left Barry's room, he called me to one side and said to me, "Im so sorry" It's only a matter of hours now! I stood there rooted to the spot, i couldn't take it in. My Barry was going to die, and soon. As i saw him out, he said to me that he wasn't on duty that night, but he would leave his bleeper on in case i needed him. What do i do, i was still hearing an echo, telling me that my son was on his last breath, only hours.

I rang my sister Teresa, and told her if anyone wanted to see Barry, then they had better come then, because i didn't know how long he had left! Within the hour, everyone was there, with one exception, my brother Harry. He had wanted to come down the early hours of the morning, stinking drunk, and i told him no, not a chance, then he started ranting at me, telling me i couldn't stop him, 'Oh yes i can, and i will'. In the end, my then brother-in-law, Barry Malone offered to go and pick him up from Birmingham. He took my son Tony with him on the Saturday morning. He said it wouldn't take long, only a couple of hours. I had lain next to Barry as the life was ebbing away from him. My beloved fuckin mother came in the room, and threw her arms around Barry, wailing how much she loved him, but i couldn't bear the thought of her being near him, so i told my sister Carol, "Fuckin get her out of here, So help me god, how i wished it were her and not my son, "fuckin get her away from him". At two o'clock that day, two nurses came and set a morphine pump up for Barry, but he wouldn't touch it, so they then proceeded to try and make him comfortable, but he was getting too distressed, so they left him. As they were leaving, they called me to one side and told me that my son's death was imminent, so i ran into him and told everyone except his own family to let me have some time with my baby, before i lost him. I watched the colour drain from him, starting with his fingernails, his head on my shoulder as one tear fell from his eye onto my right cheek, which to this day, still burns from time to time. The only person i let in the room, was Steve, and that was because i didn't know at that time, that the noise i heard coming from Barry's throat was what they call the death rattle, then Steve said to me, "He's going Margaret. He's free now i said, No more pain. I watched with horror as my baby had left this cruel joke of a world and went to a better one. I don't think i could have hated anyone, the way i hated myself, because i had convinced myself that i had killed him, he was the brightest star in the sky that night. MY BABY LOST HIS BATTLE FOR LIFE.

7TH DECEMBER AT 2-15PM 1996

GOODNIGHT AND GODBLESS BAZ.

Printed in July 2019
by Rotomail Italia S.p.A., Vignate (MI) - Italy